Dog-eared

Dog-eared

POEMS
ABOUT HUMANITY'S
BEST FRIEND

Edited and selected by **DUNCAN WU**

BASIC BOOKS

New York

Basic Books
Hachette Book Group
1290 Avenue of the Americas, New York, NY 10104
www.basicbooks.com

Printed in the United States of America

First Edition: October 2020

Published by Basic Books, an imprint of Perseus Books, LLC, a subsidiary of Hachette Book Group, Inc. The Basic Books name and logo is a trademark of the Hachette Book Group.

The Hachette Speakers Bureau provides a wide range of authors for speaking events. To find out more, go to www.hachettespeakersbureau.com or call (866) 376-6591.

The publisher is not responsible for websites (or their content) that are not owned by the publisher.

Print book interior design by Amy Quinn

Library of Congress Cataloging-in-Publication Data
Names: Wu, Duncan, editor.
Title: Dog-eared : poems about humanity's best friend / edited and selected by Duncan Wu.
Description: First edition. | New York : Basic Books, 2020.
Identifiers: LCCN 2020014018 | ISBN 9781541672932 (hardcover) | ISBN 9781541672918 (ebook)
Subjects: LCSH: Dogs—Poetry.
Classification: LCC PN6110.D6 D64 2020 | DDC 808.81/9362—dc23
LC record available at https://lccn.loc.gov/2020014018

ISBNs: 978-1-5416-7293-2 (hardcover), 978-1-5416-7291-8 (ebook)

LSC-C

10 9 8 7 6 5 4 3 2 1

CONTENTS

Contents

Contents

Contents

Contents

Contents

Contents

Contents

INTRODUCTION

Duncan Wu

WHY POETRY? THERE is much fiction and nonfiction about dogs, but poetry, being more compressed, can deliver more effectively that emotional jolt I'm looking for. I want to read something about a dog and be moved to laugh or cry, and poetry is the medium through which emotion works most powerfully. If you doubt that, take a look at William Stafford's "How It Began" (p. 213) or Toi Derricotte's "The Good Old Dog" (p. 239). I want the poet to hurl me against the window of the imagination and compel me to stare in horror or disbelief or wonder at the unfolding drama on the other side. I want to forget myself and be immersed in someone else's world.

This isn't the first book of its kind; anthologists have been compiling canine collections for decades. One approach is to gather together heartwarming, escapist verse that shows what incorrigible scoundrels dogs can be, but that's not the idea behind *Dog-eared*. Readers in the twenty-first century want something firmer-edged, with a foothold in the world of tough breaks and hard knocks— poetry from a world recognizably our own. Some dog poems too readily lose sight of the bestiality of their subject. The animal they describe doesn't seem like a creature that could roll in excrement; it is instead an ersatz dog—not real, but a hurried squiggle with doggy features—constructed and styled to satisfy the appetite for cuteness.

Such poems are problematic because they flatter dogs and flatter us. And they have an inbuilt tendency to veer rapidly into the realm of kitsch. We should not forget that our ancestors, as well as people today, have shown cruelty toward dogs to the point of terrible violence. Bear-baiting was practiced in England up to the nineteenth century. Bears suffered the most, but many dogs were also killed or injured. Only in 1835 did Parliament pass a law outlawing bear-baiting, though baits continued in various parts of Britain until 1842. The prohibition didn't stop people from engaging in other acts of cruelty, like tying fireworks to dogs' tails for "fun," and in fact gave impetus to the demand for dogfighting, which continues to this day in various countries.[1]

You can't build an awareness of that into your work if your dogs are carved out of polystyrene and live in Arcadia. The undeceived vision of Charles Simic is a perfect antidote. His poems are uncompromising in their determination to tell the truth; in a note written for this volume, Simic says:

> I grew up with stray dogs. It was during the Second World War in a city occupied by the Nazis and frequently bombed by the Allies where almost every street had fresh ruins, the sight of which brought misery to the grownups and joy to children and

1. Dogfighting is legal in Japan and in some parts of Russia; though illegal in most other countries, underground dogfights occur throughout much of Latin America, eastern Europe, Pakistan, Britain, and the United States.

lost dogs looking for a place to hide. Strangely, even at the age of five I was not afraid of them like other people, but would approach them even when they appeared vicious and kept barking at me as if wanting to tear me apart. Since then I don't miss an opportunity to go over to a strange dog and introduce myself. By and large they tend to be lonely creatures and so am I.

Understanding dogs as they really are is crucial to our understanding of ourselves; after all, what else are we looking at, when we reflect on our relations with dogs? Any work of art that falsifies human or canine nature has no future; only as a truth-telling medium can it have validity.

The Good Dogs

It's impossible not to feel astonished by Homer. Whether he was one person or a group of people is irrelevant to the insight "he" seems to have had into the closeness of man and dog. The story of the dog Argus stands at the beginning of this volume and has a psychological authenticity that belies its age. Its underlying conceit is that an invisible connection binds Ulysses, who has just returned home after his arduous journey, and the dog he trained as a puppy, whom he has not seen for many years. Ulysses's tragedy is shared by the dog. Returning in the guise of a beggar, he finds Argus horribly, painfully neglected, "all abjectly on the stables store" (p. 20)—lying on a pile of animal feces, covered in ticks. In this encounter the hero and his dog, reunited for the first and last time, are given something infinitely precious—a moment in which the dog is allowed the comfort of knowing his master has returned and that he is truly loved.

Up went his dog's laid ears and (coming near)
Up he himself rose, fawned, and wagged his stern,   2
Couched close his ears, and lay so. (p. 20)

The closeness of dog and owner partakes of genuine love, and that makes Ulysses and Argus a kind of touchstone, an ideal. It's the standard against which we perceive the cruelty inflicted in Baudelaire's "The Good Dogs," vivisectionist inhumanity in Browning's "Tray," and the dog's blamelessness in Andrew Motion's "The Dog of the Light Brigade." It's a vision of how things ought to be between dog and owner, and it hasn't changed in the millennia that have passed since Homer wrote his great epic.

Byron was the weirdest of men. He never knew his father, had a tortured relationship with his mother, and the only human beings he wanted to befriend were the fifteen-year-old boys with whom he constantly fell in love. His purest relationships, however, were with animals, especially dogs. He acquired Boatswain (pronounced "Bo'sun"), the Newfoundland, when he was fifteen years old in 1803. The name Boatswain was an acknowledgment of the fact that Newfoundlands were renowned for their ability to rescue people who were drowning, and Byron enjoyed putting this to the test by throwing himself off ships, Boatswain always jumping in to help him ashore. Byron was heartbroken when Boatswain died of rabies in 1808; he had nursed him to the end. He composed an epitaph that was etched in marble and erected over the dog's remains.

2. *stern* tail

But the poor dog, in life the firmest friend,
The first to welcome, foremost to defend,
Whose honest heart is still his master's own,
Who labors, fights, lives, breathes, for him alone,
Unhonored falls, unnoticed all his worth,
Denied in heaven the soul he held on earth. (p. 110)

Byron portrays the dog, much as Homer does, as the victim of neglect; in his lines Boatswain's loyalty, dedication, and love are rewarded with exclusion from heaven. The important point for Byron is that dogs are better than humans. They love where humans merely lust; they are faithful where humans are capable of betrayal.

The idea that dogs are better than people—angels with four furry legs and a tail—goes back at least to the seventeenth century, when Anne Finch ventriloquized the thoughts of the vigilant Snarl, who was capable of identifying thieves, flatterers, and even gold-digging women (pp. 63–64). The poet Robert Herrick, a huge admirer of Charles I, owned a King Charles spaniel called Tracie and wrote that, when the dog died, he would give him "one / Tear, that deserves of me a million" (p. 59). What's distinctly English about that is the restraint—the "one / Tear," which he admits immediately to be an act of meanness. Such self-awareness is both stoic and, at the same time, highly emotional because we know that, even if he does only shed one tear, he really wants to "cry a river." That seventeenth-century restraint is not only manly (at least by the standards of the time), it is also different from the more declarative manner of Byron, because it sets up the inability to adequately mourn the dog as a virtue. The superiority of dogs is also, unexpectedly, the subject of William Cowper's "On a Spaniel Called Beau, Killing a Young Bird" (p. 73). Cowper begins by thinking the dog deserves to be reprimanded, but he then writes a response in the dog's voice, in which Beau says he was only obeying the call of Nature (p. 74). For many of Cowper's readers, and certainly for most of the Romantics, that would have seemed a completely adequate response, warranting Beau's exoneration. Nature, after all, was seen as a powerful ordering force on a universal scale, not to be quarreled with.

Walking his beloved Ponto, Victor Hugo reflects on the abominable behavior of humans compared to Ponto's, who is "honesty unleashed" (p. 121)—a claim that turns the dog into a moral exemplar, something licensed quite emphatically by Hugo. Charles Baudelaire, by contrast, was not originally a great admirer of dogs, and could grumble about what disgusting creatures they were (see, for instance, "The Dog and the Perfume Bottle," p. 144). But after seeing how miserably dogs were treated in Belgium (a country he described as "a monster"), he wrote what can only be described as a sort of love letter to them, "The Good Dogs" (p. 144), which concludes by imagining "a special paradise for good dogs, poor dogs, mud-bespattered dogs, and sad dogs" (p. 148). The poem is one of the great works of French literature, and one of the most compelling works in this anthology.

In Ivan Turgenev's prose poem, "The Dog" (p. 137), the author sits with a dog and intuits, through an almost mystic insight, "that at this instant there is living in him and in me the same feeling, that there is no difference between us. We are the same; in each of us there burns and shines the same trembling spark" (p. 138). It is tempting to imagine this sense of affinity as deriving from a peculiarly Russian dislike of isolation, but, in fact, it is found in poems by writers the world over.

This growing belief that "there is no difference between us" was incompatible with vivisection, the practice of conducting experimental surgeries on living animals, which many activists, including a number of poets, began opposing in the 1870s. In Robert Browning's "Tray," published 1879, a vivisectionist threatens to slice open a dog who has saved the life of a young girl, to learn where its soul might be (p. 134). In this poem, passivity is not an option. We have either to endorse the unfortunate dog's fate, or to question it. By what standard is being sliced open while alive the appropriate reward for Tray's heroic act? That question is never explicitly stated, but there can be no dodging it. Worse still, the scientist's declared mission is to *find the soul*—as if that were possible. There is a strong underpinning of moral outrage, all part of a larger strategy to compel us to think for ourselves.

Christina Rossetti, a contemporary of Browning's and owner of a pet wombat, was also a passionate anti-vivisectionist whose poem against the practice begins with "a poor old dog / Who wags his tail a-begging in his need" (p. 158). The image may seem a little sentimental, but there was nothing sugary about it for her: there were stray, homeless dogs everywhere in Victorian London, many of whom simply died in the streets.

The poems that confront human cruelty to dogs may be among the most memorable in this volume. That preoccupation looks back to Homer and the terrible manner in which the servants in Ulysses's house neglect Argus. What makes Galway Kinnell's "Burning" worse is the efficiency with which its central character kills the "yellow hound" that saved his life (p. 225). The poem is a terrible, chilling commentary on man's unspeakable inhumanity to animals and, as with Browning's poem, it places the responsibility for some kind of judgment squarely with the reader.

The Bad Dogs

It may be harder to think of dogs as nice once you've watched them tear other animals limb from limb. The Actaeon episode in Ovid's *Metamorphoses* confronts us with a pack of dogs ready to chase down their owner, disguised as a deer, and kill him. The cleverness of the situation is that they are innocent as they do it because they have no way of knowing that the deer is their beloved Actaeon; as far as they know, this is one of many wild animals their owner has trained them to hunt for sport. Ovid revels in the irony, listing by name as many of the dogs as possible, with details of their origins.

His hounds espied him where he was, and Blackfoot first of all,
And Stalker special good of scent began aloud to call.
This latter was a hound of Crete, the other was of Sparta.
Then all the kennel fell in round, and every for his part
Did follow freshly in the chase more swifter than the wind—
Spy, Eateal, Scalecliff, three good hounds come all of
    Arcas' kind;   3
Strong Kilbuck, currish Savage, Spring, and Hunter
    fresh of smell,
And Lightfoot who to lead a chase did bear away the bell;   4
Fierce Woodman hurt not long ago in hunting of a boar,

---

3. *come* related   4. *bear away the bell* beat the others

And Shepherd wont to follow sheep and neat to field afore; 5

And Laund, a fell and eager bitch that had a wolf to sire; 6

Another brach called Greedigut with two her puppies by her; 7

And Ladon gaunt as any greyhound, a hound in Sicyon bred;

Blab, Fleetwood, Patch whose necked skin with sundry
　　spots was spread;

Wight, Bowman, Royster (beauty fair and white as
　　winter's snow),

And Tawny full of dusky hairs that over all did grow;

With lusty Ruffler passing all the residue there in strength, 8

And Tempest best of footmanship in holding out at length;

And Cole, and Swift, and little Wolf, as wight as any other, 9

Accompanied with a Cyprian hound that was his
　　native brother, 10

And Snatch amid whose forehead stood a star as white
　　as snow,

The residue being all as black and slick as any crow;

And shaggy Rug with other twain that had a sire of Crete

And dam of Sparta, one of them called Jollyboy, a great

And large-flewd hound, the other Chorle who ever
　　gnoorring went, 11

And Ringwood with a shyrle loud mouth the which he
　　freely spent, 12

With divers mo whose names to tell it were but loss of time.
　　(p. 24–26) 13

5. *neat* cows   6. *fell* fierce   7. *brach* bitch   8. *passing* exceeding   9. *wight*
energetic   10. *Cyrian* from Cyprus   11. *flewd* lipped; *gnoorring* snarling
12. *shyrle* rough   13. *mo* more

These are the bad dogs par excellence. For Ovid, their naming *is* poetry—and a marvelous way of building suspense. As we read these lines, we begin to realize what an impossible challenge the deer has in outrunning his pursuers, and how carefully the hunting pack was assembled in the first place—by the very man it is to destroy. While these realities sink in, Ovid enumerates details that do not contribute in any way to the narrative, other than to embellish the horror that is about to unfold.

These were some of the best bad dogs of the Elizabethan period, and their influence is felt throughout subsequent literature. Geoffrey Chaucer, that genius of medieval storytelling, had already amused himself with the names of the dogs who pursue the fox in "The Nun's Priest's Tale" ("Ran Colle oure dogge, and Talbot and Gerland," p. 40), and the same motif is repeated by Shakespeare in Theseus's description of a hunt:

My hounds are bred out of the Spartan kind, [14]
So flewed, so sanded, and their heads are hung
With ears that sweep away the morning dew;
Crook-kneed, and dewlapped like Thessalian bulls;
Slow in pursuit, but matched in mouth like bells,
Each under each. A cry more tuneable [15]
Was never holla'd to, nor cheered with horn
In Crete, in Sparta, nor in Thessaly:
Judge when you hear. (p. 53)

14. *kind* lineage   15. *tuneable* musical

The baddest of the bad must be Cowper's Beau, already mentioned above under the rubric of good dogs. But regardless of what Cowper has him say, he is a killer; everything he says is a justification of cold-blooded murder—which he claims, speciously or not, to be a call of Nature. The dog in Hannah More's "Patient Joe" (p. 79) is hardly better—an unrepentant thief who steals others' lunches whenever the chance arises, even if, as in the poem, the theft has an unexpectedly positive outcome. More's focus is not on the dog, but like all tragic storytellers, she has a keen sense of irony—and in this case the poem's resolution is entirely canine.

There is irony of a more refined sort in Thomas Hardy's stunning, "Ah, Are You Digging on My Grave?" (p. 164). Its premise is shocking: the poem's speaker is a corpse, a woman in a grave recently disturbed by digging. The dead woman asks, "Then, who is digging on my grave?" She runs through the various possibilities until a voice provides the answer:

Oh it is I, my mistress dear,
Your little dog, who still lives near,
And much I hope my movements here
Have not disturbed your rest?

The stage is set for an affectionate reunion: Oh yes, the corpse says, my nice doggie is "that one true heart" who remembers me— hooray for "a dog's fidelity!" Most eighteenth-century writers would have ended the poem there, but Hardy's genius is to sniff out the opportunity for a cruel punch line, which the speaking dog delivers, holding nothing back:

Mistress, I dug upon your grave
To bury a bone, in case
I should be hungry near this spot
When passing on my daily trot.
I am sorry, but I quite forgot
It was your resting-place.

Hardy's genius lies in that innocent phrase, "I am sorry." Perhaps the dog *is* sorry, but his politeness cannot blind us to the unhappy realization that the corpse's ecstatic celebration of canine fidelity is utterly unfounded. And the playful rhyme with "trot" underlines how unserious the dog is in his daily return to "this spot." Hardy does not relate the corpse's reaction to this breathtaking response: we have to imagine her, lying for eternity, six feet underground, knowing that her only visitor will be a dog who uses her grave for his bone-burying. She is otherwise forgotten. Perhaps it is funny— but it is also designed to make us feel distinctly queasy.

Exactly the same discomfort pervades Charles Simic's "Icarus's Dog" (p. 232) in which the dog bears witness to his master's death before acting in a persuasively doggy manner: "Now and then stopping to pee / And take one more look at the sky." Simic is too humane a writer to give this the cold edge we find in Hardy; he is more concerned with describing how dogs think and behave. Unlike humans, dogs do not aspire to emotional states they think they ought to feel; they do as they want.

Dogs as They Truly Are

Hardy's is the first dog in this book who speaks exactly as one would expect. In the twentieth century there are an increasing number that behave in an identifiably doggy manner. William Carlos Williams's "Smell!" (p. 188) gives us a dog "indiscriminately" smelling every possible odor during a walk. "Can you not be decent? Can you not reserve your ardors / for something less unlovely?," Williams asks. Well, no, is the implied answer—because (as Cowper might say) that is Nature's way. Dorothy Parker, in "Verse for a Certain Dog" (p. 204), reprimands a pet who eats biscuits on her bed, threatens to knock over the fishbowl, and enjoys using the kitten as a basketball—not by any means the most troublesome of dogs, but a recognizably mischievous one who we know will simply disregard everything she says.

That most intelligent of poets (and one of the most shamefully neglected), Howard Nemerov, reflects on his affinities with the dog he walks each day in "Walking the Dog" (p. 221). He and his mutt are, he says, two universes "connected by love and a leash and nothing else." He refines that observation by saying they are also connected by "our interest in shit"—one of the most honest comments in this book because it incriminates not just the dog, but us too. Nemerov is nothing if not honest—and it may be that unless one is prepared to be as honest as he is, there is little point in writing poetry at all.

Craig Raine is as uncompromising as anyone when it comes to looking things in the face, and his three poems here bear that out. But while rubbing our noses in uncomfortable truths, he also wants to make us laugh:

they scratch their itches

like one-legged cyclists sprinting
for home, pee like hurdlers,

shit like weightlifters, and relax
by giving each other piggy backs . . . ("The Behaviour of Dogs,"
  p. 245)

Once again, there's something very English about this kind of truth-telling. The physical functions Raine describes are not things we might want to imagine, but his language, which is at once figurative and unstrained, is not only pleasurable to read, but also funny. His clever use of rhyme has something to do with this—"relax" and "piggy backs" being especially effective.

    A. E. Stallings has a lighter touch, but she too is interested in the dogginess of dogs. In the final poem in this anthology she imagines a dog from ancient Greece, finding it no different from any other, even as it is ferried across the River Styx by Charon:

In the press for the ferry, who will lift her into the boat?
Will she cower under the pier and be forgotten,
Forever howling and whimpering, tail tucked under?
What stranger pays her passage? (p. 261)

And with that, Stallings gives flesh to what was no more than a skeleton; the dog becomes real because of the way it is character-ized. "Will she cower under the pier and be forgotten"? The dog's behavior in the face of the unknown is true to our experience of dogs—and that's what Stallings needs to give depth to her conception.

A shake as she scrambles ashore sets the beads jingling.
And then, that last, tense moment—touching noses
Once, twice, three times, with unleashed Cerberus. (p. 262)

Stallings has watched dogs closely and noted how they touch noses on meeting, so she imagines her dog greeting each of Cerberus's three heads. That's a touch of genius. Not only is it true, it is also very funny.

When poets describe dogs truthfully, it's almost impossible not to be drawn in by their otherness, yet the paradox is that all good dog poems are essentially about us, not them. And great poets seem instinctively to understand how dogs reflect our fears, obsessions, and needs. Perhaps that's why I credit the poets who synthesize the canine perspective most persuasively, even as they write about themselves.

NOTE ON TEXTS

STANDARDS AND CONVENTIONS concerning punctuation, cap-
italization, and other incidentals of the text have altered signifi-
cantly over the centuries. In the case of poems edited from early
printed or manuscript sources, I have seen fit to punctuate, or
repunctuate, in a manner that preserves the meaning and integrity
of the original while making the poem accessible to the modern
reader.

HOMER

(750 BC–650 BC)

Translated by George Chapman

VERY LITTLE IS known about Homer—we do not even know whether he was one person or several. And if he was blind, as is often claimed, someone must have helped him with the task of writing. One thing we do know: he (or they) had a faultless sense of drama, and that was never clearer than in this extract from the *Odyssey*, Book 17, well after the end of the Trojan War. For this extract I have turned to one of the most sensitive of Homer's English translators, the Elizabethan poet George Chapman (1559–1634), whose 1616 rendering so delighted John Keats and inspired his sonnet "On first reading Chapman's Homer."

After years of struggle, Ulysses has arrived home to find the "suitors" partying every night at his expense—all 108 of whom are trying to persuade his wife, Penelope, to marry them. Disguised as a beggar, he is accompanied by Eumaeus, a swineherd who is one of his slaves. Eumaeus still does not know Ulysses's identity, but Argus, the dog he reared from puppyhood, knows Ulysses immediately, greets him, wagging his tail for the last time. The earliest dog-poem in this anthology thus tells the tale of canine affection and fidelity.

Odyssey, Book 17 (extract)

    when in the yard there lay
A dog called Argus which, before his way
Assumed for Ilion, Ulysses bred [1]
Yet stood his pleasure then in little stead
(As being too young) but growing to his grace [2]
Young men made choice of him for every chase; [3]
Or of their wild goats, of their hares or harts.
But his King gone, and he now past his parts, [4]
Lay all abjectly on the stables store, [5]
Before the ox-stall, and mules' stable-door,
To keep the clothes, cast from the peasants' hands,
While they laid compost on Ulysses' lands:
The dog, with ticks (unlooked-to) overgrown. [6]
But by this dog no sooner seen but known
Was wise Ulysses, who new-entered there:
Up went his dog's laid ears and (coming near)
Up he himself rose, fawned, and wagged his stern, [7]
Couched close his ears, and lay so—nor discern [8]
Could evermore his dear-loved Lord again.
Ulysses saw it, nor had power to abstain
From shedding tears, which (far-off seeing his swain)
He dried from his sight clean; to whom he thus

1. **bred** trained   2. **grace**, i.e., fine hunting ability   3. **chase** hunt   4. **past his parts**, i.e., aged, incapable   5. **store**, i.e., of animal feces   6. **unlooked-to** untreated; **overgrown** covered   7. **stern** tail   8. **Couched close** lowered

His grief dissembled: "'Tis miraculous   9
That such a dog as this should have his lair
On such a dunghill, for his form is fair.
And yet I know not if there were in him
Good pace or parts, for all his goodly limn.   10
Or he lived empty of those inward things,
As are those trencher-beagles, tending kings,   11
Whom for their pleasures or their glories ache,
Or fashion, they into their favours take."
"This dog," said he, "was servant to one dead
A huge time since. But if he bore his head
(For form and quality) of such a height,
As when Ulysses (bound for the Ilion fight,
Or quickly after) left him, your rapt eyes   12
Would then admire to see him use his thighs   13
In strength and swiftness. He would nothing fly   14
Nor anything let escape. If once his eye
Seized any wild beast, he knew straight his scent;   15
Go where he would, away with him he went.
Nor was there ever any savage stood   16
Amongst the thickets of the deepest wood
Long time before him, but he pulled him down;
As well by that true hunting to be shown
In such vast coverts as for speed of pace
In any open lawn; for in deep chase,   17

9. *dissembled* disguised   10. *pace or parts* good abilities; *limn* appearance
11. *trencher-beagles* pet dogs   12. *rapt* entranced   13. *admire* be struck with
admiration   14. *fly* flee   15. *straight* instantly   16. *savage* wild beast   17. *lawn*
glade

He was a passing wise and well-nosed hound.
And yet is all this good in him uncrowned
With any grace here now, nor he more fed   [18]
Then any errant cur. His King is dead   [19]
Far from his country, and his servants are
So negligent, they lend his hound no care.
Where masters rule not, but let men alone
You never there see honest service done.
That man's half virtue, Jove takes quite away,
That once is sunburned with the servile day."   [20]
This said, he entered the well-builded towers,
Up bearing right upon the glorious wooers
And left poor Argus dead. His lord's first sight
Since that time twenty years bereft his light.   [21]

18. *grace* recognition   19. *errant cur* badly behaved, worthless dog   20. *That man's half-virtue . . . servile day*, i.e., the experience of being someone's slave strips a man of even the little virtue he may possess.   21. *bereft his light*, i.e., led to his sudden death

OVID

(43 BC–AD 17)

Translated by Arthur Golding

PUBLIUS OVIDIUS NASO was a Roman poet born to a well-to-do family in 43 BC, a year after Julius Caesar's assassination. He wanted to be a poet from an early age and composed what was to be his greatest work, the fifteen-book *Metamorphoses*, between 2 BC and AD 8. I have included the story of the hunter Actaeon and his dogs, who have always been the stars of this episode. The tale is best known to British readers in the translation of the Elizabethan writer, Arthur Golding (1535–1606). Shakespeare was an enthusiastic reader of Golding, and the speeches from *A Midsummer Night's Dream* (4. 1) below (p. 52) are certainly influenced by the lines included here.

Actaeon accidentally stumbles across the goddess Diana, bathing naked in the woods with her ladies-in-waiting. Although he is as much a victim of circumstance as they are, he is promptly cursed by Diana to be turned into a deer and hunted down and torn to shreds by his own dogs. Later translators such as Ted Hughes have chosen to emphasize Actaeon's innocence. Golding instead seems fixated by the brutal injustice meted out to Actaeon, naming and counting off each hunting-dog and describing with relish his slow, unpleasant death with a relish embodied in the painful description of his slow, unpleasant death from the dogs' "greedy teeth and griping paws." The extract below begins as Diana throws water over Actaeon, turning him into a hart.

Metamorphoses, Book 3 (extract)

So raught the water in her hands, and for to wreak the spite,   1

Besprinkled all the head and face of the unlucky Knight,

And thus forespake the heavy lot that should upon him light.   2

"Now make thy vaunt among thy mates, thou saw'st

     Diana bare.   3

Tell if thou can, I give thee leave, tell hardly, do not spare."   4

This done, she makes no further threats, but by and by

     doth spread

A pair of lively old hart's horns upon his sprinkled head.

She sharps his ears, she makes his neck both slender,

     long and lank.

She turns his fingers into feet, his arms to spindle-shank.   5

She wraps him in a hairy hide beset with speckled spots,

And planteth in him fearfulness—and so away he trots,

Full greatly wondering to himself what made him in that case   6

To be so wight and swift of foot. But when he saw his face   7

And horned temples in the brook, he would have cried "Alas!",

But as for then no kind of speech out of his lips could pass.

1. *raught* held   2. *forespake* predicted; *lot* fate   3. *vaunt* boast   4. *hardly* loudly   5. *spindle-shank* a long, slender leg   6. *case* instance   7. *wight* strong

He sight and brayed—for that was then the speech that
   did remain,   8
And down the eyes that were not his, his bitter tears did rain.
No part remained (save his mind) of that he erst had been.   9
What should he do? Turn home again to Cadmus and
   the Queen?
Or hide himself among the woods? Of this he was afraid,
And of the tother ill ashamed.

                       While doubting thus he stayed:
His hounds espied him where he was, and Blackfoot first of all,
And Stalker special good of scent began aloud to call.
This latter was a hound of Crete, the other was of Sparta.
Then all the kennel fell in round, and every for his part
Did follow freshly in the chase more swifter than the wind—
Spy, Eateal, Scalecliff, three good hounds come all of
   Arcas' kind;   10
Strong Kilbuck, currish Savage, Spring, and Hunter fresh
   of smell,
And Lightfoot who to lead a chase did bear away the bell;   11
Fierce Woodman hurt not long ago in hunting of a boar,
And Shepherd wont to follow sheep and neat to field afore;   12
And Laund, a fell and eager bitch that had a wolf to sire;   13
Another brach called Greedigut with two her puppies by her;   14
And Ladon gaunt as any greyhound, a hound in Sicyon bred;
Blab, Fleetwood, Patch whose necked skin with sundry spots
   was spread;

8. *sight* saw   9. *save* except; *erst* formerly   10. *come* related   11. *bear away the bell* beat the others   12. *neat* cows   13. *fell* fierce   14. *brach* bitch

Wight, Bowman, Royster (beauty fair and white as
    winter's snow),
And Tawny full of dusky hairs that over all did grow;
With lusty Ruffler passing all the residue there in strength,   15
And Tempest best of footmanship in holding out at length;
And Cole, and Swift, and little Wolf, as wight as any other,   16
Accompanied with a Cyprian hound that was his
    native brother,   17
And Snatch amid whose forehead stood a star as white
    as snow,
The residue being all as black and slick as any crow;
And shaggy Rug with other twain that had a sire of Crete
And dam of Sparta, one of them called Jollyboy, a great
And large-flewd hound, the other Chorle who ever gnoorring
    went,   18
And Ringwood with a shyrle loud mouth the which he freely
    spent,   19
With divers mo whose names to tell it were but loss of time.   20
This fellows over hill and dale in hope of pray do climb,   21
Through thick and thin and craggy cliffs where was no
    way to go,
He flies through grounds where oftentimes he chaséd had
    ere tho,   22
Even from his own folk is he fain (alas!) to flee away;
He strained oftentimes to speak, and was about to say
"I am Actaeon: know your Lord and Master, sirs, I pray!"

15. *passing* exceeding   16. *wight* energetic   17. *Cyrian* from Cyprus
18. *flewd* lipped; *gnoorring* snarling   19. *shyrle* rough   20. *mo* more   21. *pray* prayer   22. *ere tho* before then

But use of words and speech did want to utter forth his mind.   23
Their cry did ring through all the wood redoubled with
    the wind.
First Slo did pinch him by the haunch, and next came
    Kildeer in,
And Hylbred fastened on his shoulder, bit him through
    the skin.
These came forth later than the rest, but coasting thwart a hill,   24
They did gaincope him as he came, and held their Master still,   25
Until that all the rest came in, and fastened on him too.
No part of him was free from wound; he could none other do
But sigh, and in the shape of hart with voice as harts are wont,
(For voice of man was none now left to help him at the brunt)   26
By braying show his secret grief among the mountains high,
And kneeling sadly on his knees with dreary tears in eye,
As one by humbling of himself that mercy seemed to crave,
With piteous look instead of hands his head about to wave.
Not knowing that it was their Lord, the huntsmen cheer
    their hounds
With wonted noise and for Actaeon look about the grounds;
They "halloo!" who could loudest cry, still calling him by name,
As though he were not there, and much his absence they
    do blame
In that he came not to the fall, but slacked to see the game.   27
As often as they named him he sadly shook his head,
And fain he would have been away thence in some other stead;

---

23. *want* lack   24. *coasting* crossing   25. *gaincope* intercept   26. *brunt* attack
(of the dogs)   27. *Slacked* neglected

But there he was. And well he could have found in heart to see
His dogs' fell deeds, so that to feel in place he had not been.
They hem him in on every side, and in the shape of Stag,
With greedy teeth and griping paws their Lord in pieces drag.

CRINAGORAS

(ca. 1st century AD)

Translated by Gideon Nisbet

CRINAGORAS WAS BORN on the Greek island of Mytilene, capital city and port on the island of Lesbos, and was sent as Greek ambassador to Rome, where he wrote the epigrams that are now part of the *Greek Anthology*.

Dog Avoidance Tactics

"Each to his trade": beneath the Alpine peaks
The shaggy bandits with their spiky hair
Pursue their larceny and still avoid
The dogs of their pursuers, by this means:
They take a kidney, rub it on themselves
Till every bit of fat is on their skin.
Its pungent odour fools the keen-nosed hounds.
You savants of Liguria, inclined
More to devise the wicked than the good.

MARTIAL (MARCUS VALERIUS MARTIALIS)

(between AD 38/41 and ca. 104)

Translated by Duncan Wu

MARTIAL WAS A Spanish-born inhabitant of Rome and proba-
bly the greatest (and rudest) of the Roman satirists. His poetry is
strongly influenced by that of Catullus (ca. 84–54 BC) and pokes
fun at the social lives of well-to-do Romans, including their atti-
tudes toward dogs. The epigram about Issa is the first poem in this
book that is concerned with a lapdog rather than a hunting-dog.
Publius, Roman governor of Malta, was Issa's proud owner.

Epigram 1.83

Your cute little pup licks your face and lips;
Oh what a surprise!—he loves to eat shit.

Epigram 1.109

Issa is a bigger scamp than Catullus's
Sparrow—purer than the peck of a dove;
More seductive than any louche slave-girl;
More precious than strings of Indian pearls:
Issa, darling lapdog of Publius.

He hears her speak in her croons; she knows when
He's happy or sad; she slumbers, her snout
On his neck, so soundly he can't hear her
Breathing. When her bladder's full to bursting,
She won't let a drop touch the sheets, instead
Nudging him with her pawpad so that, when
Roused, he sets her on the floor, and lifts her
Back on the bed when she's done. Innately
Chaste and modest, she's a stranger to love,
No mate being equal to the tender
Young bitch. Lest the Grim Reaper remove all
Trace of her, Publius paints her portrait
Which is more lifelike than the dog herself:
Place them side by side, and you would suppose
Both the real thing or both works of art.

ST ALDHELM, ABBOT OF MALMESBURY AND BISHOP OF SHERBORNE
(d. 709/710)
Translated by Duncan Wu

THE FIRST CHRISTIAN author in this volume, Aldhelm was the author of both letters and poetry, including a hundred riddles in verse, the *Enigmata*.

On the Hound

The holy power that long since made me
Set me to chase my master's evil foes.
I wage war with weapons in my jaws, though
At home I retreat from the blows of brats.

LI BAI
(701–762)

Translated by Stephen Owen

Li Bai was an extraordinary character in Chinese literature. Said to be partly of Turkish descent, he seems to have lived in his earlier years as an *avant la lettre* Cyrano de Bergerac, redressing evils wherever he found them. Rejecting a life of respectability, he refused to take the examinations that would have enabled him to follow a career in the civil service. Despite that, he remained throughout his life an enthusiastic student of physics and chemistry. In the poem below, written in 718, the barking of a dog is the first in a series of observations that confirm absence—most obviously that of a reclusive Tao master. It is as if the barking is a kind of static that interferes with the possibility of enlightenment—a concept Li Bai might have been skeptical about.

Visiting the Recluse on Mount Tai Tian and Not Finding Him In

A dog barks amid the sound of waters,
Peach blossoms dark, bearing dew.
Where trees are thickest, sometimes see a deer,

And when noon strikes the ravine, hear no bell.
Bamboo of wilderness split through blue haze,
A cascade in flight, hung from an emerald peak
But no one knows where you've gone—
Disappointed, I linger among these few pines.

ANONYMOUS, *THE SEERESS'S PROPHECY*

(10th century)

Translated by Carolyne Larrington

THE *POETIC EDDA* records stories from the mythic pagan culture of Iceland and Norway, and most of its poems derive from a single manuscript, retained today in Reykjavik. Its Old Norse cosmos features Yggdrasill, an ash-tree of huge proportions, whose roots penetrate deep into the earth, as well as Hel, where the dead are to be found. The *Edda* comprises a number of poems including *The Seeress's Prophecy*, testament of a prophetess who remembers the beginning of the world and can see ahead to Ragnarok, the Doom of the Gods. The brief extract below describes a recurring vision of Garm, the supernatural canine monster whose barking signals the end of the world. Garm may be related to the pup that guards the way to Hel's realm. As Odin, chief of the gods, journeys there to discover why his son Baldr is having evil dreams, he is intercepted by a younger beast:

2. he met there a pup, come straight out of hell.
3. Blood there was all over its chest

long it barked
at the father of spells [1]

The Seeress's Prophecy (extract)

44. Loud Garm barks in front of Gnipa-cave,
the fetter will fray and the fierce one run free,
she knows many wise things, I see into the future
to the dread, mighty fate of the victory-gods.
45. Brother fights brother and brings his death,
Close kin destroy their blood-bonds;
It's hard in the world, adultery is rife,
An age of axes, age of swords, shields smash apart,
Age of wind, age of wolves, until the world spins downwards;
No man gives another one quarter.
46. Mim's sons cavort and the Measuring-Tree kindles
As the old Giallar-horn resounds;
Heimdall blows it loudly, holds his horn aloft. [2]
Odin consults Mim's head.
47. Yggdrasill shakes, the ash-tree standing tall,
the old tree moans and the giant has got free;
On the hell-ways everyone is fearful,
before Surt's kinsman engulfs it all. [3]
49. Loud Garm barks in front of Gnipa-cave,
the fetter will fray and the fierce one run free,
she knows many wise things, I see into the future
to the dread, mighty fate of the victory-gods.

1. *father of spells* Odin   2. *Heimdall* watchman of the gods   3. *Surt's kinsman* fire

GEOFFREY CHAUCER
(ca. 1340–1400)

CHAUCER WAS AN administrator, first under Edward III and then under Richard II, whom he served as a chief clerk of the king's works. He spent his working life in Aldgate, in the city of London, with his wife, Philippa, but by the time he embarked on his greatest work, *The Canterbury Tales*, he had moved to Kent. In London he would have had daily contact with dogs, who provided a sort of four-legged waste disposal service, free at point of access. A number of lapdogs play an important role in the characterization of the fastidious, vaguely louche Prioress, Mistress Eglentyne, in *The Canterbury Tales*:

Of smale houndes hadde she, that she fedde
With rosted flessh, or milk and wastel-breed.   1
But soore wepte she if oon of hem were deed,
Or if men smoot it with a yerde smerte;   2
And al was conscience, and tendre herte. (146–150)

1. *wastel-breed* finely made bread   2. *smoot* hit; *yerde* stick

The most memorable dogs in Chaucer are those in "The Nun's Priest's Tale," an essential part of the rescue team summoned to foil Reynard the fox's attempted raid on the residence of Chanticleer the cock and his numerous concubines.

The Nun's Priest's Tale (extract)

This sely wydwe and eek hir doghtres two,   3
Herden thise hennes crie and maken wo,
And out at dores stirten they anon,
And syen the fox toward the grove gon,   4
And bar upon his bak the cok away,   5
And cryden, "Out, harrow, and weylaway!   6
Ha! ha! The fox!" and after hym they ran,
And eek with staves many another man,   7
Ran Colle oure dogge, and Talbot and Gerland,
And Malkyn with a distaf in hir hand;
Ran cow and calf, and eek the verray hogges,   8
So fered for berking of the dogges   9
And shouting of the men and wommen eek,
They ronne so, hem thoughte hir herte breeke.   10
They yolleden as feendes doon in helle;   11
The dokes cryden as men wolde hem quelle;   12
The gees for feere flowen over the trees;   13
Out of the hive cam the swarm of bees.
So hidous was the noyse—ah, benedicitee!   14

3. *sely* good, humble   4. *syen* saw   5. *bar* carried   6. *harrow* help   7. *staves* sticks   8. *eek* also   9. *fered* afraid; Very frightened because of the barking dogs.   10. *breeke* broke   11. *yolleden* yelled; *doon* do   12. *dokes* ducks; The ducks cried as if men were killing them.   13. *flowen* flew away   14. *benedicitee!* bless us!

Certes, he Jakke Straw and his meynee 15

Ne made nevere shoutes half so shrille,

Whan that they wolden any Flemyng kille, 16

As thilke day was maad upon the fox. 17

Of bras they broghten bemes, and of box, 18

Of horn, of boon, in whiche they blewe and powped, 19

And therwithal they shriked and they howped: 20

It semed as that hevene sholde falle!

15. *meynee* followers   16. Jack Straw was one of three leaders of the Peasants'
Revolt of 1381, an uprising in which workers demanded more favorable terms of
taxation from the government. During the revolt, a mob chased and killed Flemish
workers from the continent. This is one of Chaucer's rare allusions to what for him
was contemporary history.   17. *thilke* that   18. *bemes* trumpets; *box* boxwood
19. *boon* bone; *powped* tooted   20. *howped* whooped

JOHN HEYWOOD
(b. 1496/7, d. in or after 1578)

HEYWOOD WAS A playwright and epigrammist. Although he began his career as a singer in the court of Henry VIII, he later became a playwright and is better known as such. The epigram below is the first instance of the phrase "Love me, love my dog," one of the most memorable in this collection.

Of Loving a Dog

Love me, love my dog: by love to agree,
I love thy dog as well as I love thee.

GEORGE TURBERVILLE
(b. 1543/4, d. in or after 1597)

EDUCATED FIRST AT Winchester then at New College, Oxford, Turberville moved on to the Inns of Court before making his name as a translator of Ovid, and as a poet in his own right. He was, apparently, a spaniel-owner.

To his Love that controlled his Dog for fawning on her

Indeed, my dear, you wrong my dog in this,
And show yourself to be of crabbéd kind,
That will not let my fawning whelp to kiss
Your fist, that fain would show his master's mind:
A mastiff were more fit for such a one
That cannot let her lover's dog alone.

He in his kind for me did seem to sue
That erst did stand so highly in your grace,   1
His master's mind the witty spaniel knew,
And thought his wonted mistress was in place:

1. *erst* once, formerly

45

But now at last (good faith!) I plainly see
That dogs more wise than women friendly be.

Wherefore since you so cruelly entreat
My whelp, not forcing of his fawning cheer,
You show yourself with pride to be replete,
And to your friend your nature doth appear:
The proverb old is verified in you,
"Love me and love my dog"—and so adieu.

Both I and he, that sely beast, sustain   2
For loving well and bearing faithful hearts,
Despitous checks, and rigorous disdain,   3
Where both have well deservéd for our parts:
For friendship I, for offered service he—
And yet thou neither lov'st the dog nor me.

2. *sely* humble, innocent   3. ***Despitous*** insulting; ***rigorous*** cruel

SIR JOHN HARINGTON
(bap. 1560, d. 1612)

HE WAS GODSON of Elizabeth I, inventor of the first flushing lav-
atory (which he called Ajax), and translator of Ludovico Ariosto's
epic poem, *Orlando Furioso*. If these two epigrams are anything
to go by, he may also have been a dog-beating, wife-bullying, tin-
pot dictator—though it should be remembered that he did have a
favorite dog, Bungey, immortalized in a portrait preserved at An-
glesey Abbey, Cambridgeshire, in England. Bungey was known to
take Harington's letters to correspondents more than a hundred
miles away.

To his Wife, for Striking her Dog
Your little dog that barked as I came by,
I struck by hap so hard I made him cry;   1
And straight you put your finger in your eye
And louring sat, and asked the reason why.
"Love me and love my dog," thou didst reply,
"Love as both should be loved." "I will," said I,
And sealed it with a kiss. There by and by

1. *hap* accident

Cleared were the clouds of thy fair-frowning sky.
Thus small events great masteries may try;
  For I by this do at their meaning guess
  That beat a whelp before a lioness.

To my Lady Rogers of Breaking her Bitch's Leg

Last night you laid it, Madam, in our dish,
How that a maid of ours (whom we must check)
Had broke your bitch's leg; I straight did wish
The baggage rather broken had her neck:
You took my answer well and all was whish.   2
  But take me right; I meant in that I said,
  Your baggage bitch, and not my baggage maid.

2. *whish* quiet

WILLIAM SHAKESPEARE
(1564–1616)

"THE CAT WILL mew and dog will have his day" (*Hamlet*, 5.1.287).
Shakespeare would have seen dogs scavenging on the mean streets
of Cheapside and Southwark, before Britons had committed them-
selves to the pet-based culture that prevails today. Consequently,
he tends to invoke dogs unfavorably: Richard III is a "bloody dog";
Lear calls Oswald a "whoreson dog"; Lear's daughters are "dog
hearted"; while Shylock is a "cut-throat dog." In a more extended
consideration of canine qualities, Macbeth compares hired assas-
sins with different breeds:

Ay, in the catalogue ye go for men;
As hounds and greyhounds, mongrels, spaniels, curs,
Shoughs, water-rugs, and demi-wolves, are clept
All by the name of dogs: the valu'd file
Distinguishes the swift, the slow, the subtle,
The housekeeper, the hunter, every one
According to the gift which bounteous nature
Hath in him clos'd. (*Macbeth*, 3.1.91–98)

This is not very different from the sense in which Mark Antony says the spirit of the dead Caesar "Shall in these confines with a monarch's voice / Cry Havoc and let slip the dogs of war" (*Julius Caesar*, 3.1.273), for in both instances dogs describe unprincipled, bloodthirsty humans. But there are at least three dogs who emerge with greater credit in Shakespeare, including Silver, a hunting-dog hailed by the Lord in the Induction to *The Taming of the Shrew*:

Saw'st thou not, boy, how Silver made it good
At the hedge corner, in the coldest fault?
I would not lose the dog for twenty pound. (Induction.1.17–19)

There is also the dog brought onstage by Starveling in *A Midsummer Night's Dream*, a performer in the playlet presented to Theseus; and then there is Crab, Launce's dog in *The Two Gentlemen of Verona*. Launce thinks Crab "the sourest-natured dog that lives" (2.3.5–6) but in the scene below is ready to take the blame when Crab relieves himself under the Duke's table. (Although the speech is in prose, I have regarded it as a sort of poem—which should have the audience in tears of laughter.) For a more heroic view of dogs, turn to Theseus's speeches in the second of the extracts below.

The Two Gentlemen of Verona (4.4 extract)

Enter Launce (with his dog)
When a man's servant shall play the cur with him, look you, it goes hard: one that I brought up of a puppy; one that I saved from drowning, when three or four of his blind brothers and sisters

went to it.[1] I have taught him, even as one would say precisely, "Thus I would teach a dog." I was sent to deliver him as a present to Mistress Silvia from my master; and I came no sooner into the dining-chamber but he steps me to her trencher[2] and steals her capon's leg. O, 'tis a foul thing when a cur cannot keep[3] himself in all companies! I would have (as one should say) one that takes upon him to be a dog indeed, to be, as it were, a dog at[4] all things. If I had not had more wit than he, to take a fault upon me that he did, I think verily he had been hanged for't; sure as I live, he had suffered for't. You shall judge. He thrusts me himself into the company of three or four gentleman-like dogs under the Duke's table. He had not been there (bless the mark!) a pissing-while, but all the chamber smelt him. "Out with the dog!" says one. "What cur is that?" says another. "Whip him out" says the third. "Hang him up" says the Duke. I, having been acquainted with the smell before, knew it was Crab, and goes me to the fellow that whips the dogs: "Friend," quoth I, "you mean to whip the dog?" "Ay, marry, do I," quoth he. "You do him the more wrong," quoth I; "'twas I did the thing you wot[5] of." He makes me no more ado, but whips me out of the chamber. How many masters would do this for his servant? Nay, I'll be sworn, I have sat in the stocks for puddings he hath stolen, otherwise he had been executed; I have stood on the pillory for geese he hath killed, otherwise he had suffered for't. Thou thinkest not of this now. Nay, I remember the trick you served me when I took my leave of Madam Silvia. Did not I bid thee still mark me and do as I do? When didst thou see me heave up my leg and

---

1. **went to it** met their deaths   2. **trencher** wooden plate   3. **keep** behave properly   4. **a dog at** adept at   5. **wot** know

make water against a gentlewoman's farthingale? Didst thou ever see me do such a trick?

A Midsummer Night's Dream (4.1 extract)

Enter Theseus, Hippolyta, Egeus, and others

Theseus

Go, one of you, find out the forester;

For now our observation is performed;

And since we have the vaward of the day, 6

My love shall hear the music of my hounds.

Uncouple in the western valley; let them go; 7

Dispatch, I say, and find the forester. [*Exit an attendant.*]

We will, fair queen, up to the mountain's top,

And mark the musical confusion 8

Of hounds and echo in conjunction.

Hippolyta

I was with Hercules and Cadmus once,

When in a wood of Crete they bayed the bear

With hounds of Sparta: never did I hear

Such gallant chiding, for, besides the groves, 9

The skies, the fountains, every region near

Seemed all one mutual cry. I never heard 10

So musical a discord, such sweet thunder.

6. *vaward* early part   7. *Uncouple*: release the dogs from being leashed together, setting them loose for the chase.   8. *confusion* blending   9. *chiding* yelping
10. *mutual* common

Theseus

My hounds are bred out of the Spartan kind,   [11]

So flewed, so sanded, and their heads are hung   [12]

With ears that sweep away the morning dew;   [13]

Crook-kneed, and dewlapped like Thessalian bulls;   [14]

Slow in pursuit, but matched in mouth like bells,

Each under each. A cry more tuneable   [15]

Was never holla'd to, nor cheered with horn

In Crete, in Sparta, nor in Thessaly:

Judge when you hear. But soft, what nymphs are these?

11. *kind* lineage   12. The hounds have large jaws ("flewed") and are sandy-colored ("sanded").   13. The hounds' snouts are close to the dew on the earth.   14. The hounds have bent knees and a fold of skin under the throat.   15. *tuneable* musical

JOHN DAVIES
(ca. 1565–1618)

Against Drunkards

A man, they say, surmounts all creatures far,
Yet dogs, than some men, are more regular,
For after noon they go alone from feasts
But some men cannot: they are worse than beasts.

Who Sleeps with Dogs Shall Wake with Fleas

Who sleeps with dogs shall wake with fleas
But ladies' dogs have none of these.

WILLIAM DRUMMOND OF HAWTHORNDEN
(1585–1649)

A Scot of noble birth, Drummond lived the life of an intellectual, surrounded by French, Italian, Spanish, and English books in the draughty, sepulchral Hawthornden Castle, in the village of Lasswade in Scotland. Like Sir John Harington (see p. 47), Drummond is made uncomfortably aware of his insecurities by the attention his mistress gives "that little cur."

Of her dog

When her dear bosom clips¹

That little cur, which fawns to touch her lips,

Or when it is his hap²

To lie lapped in her lap,³

O! it grows noon with me,

With hotter-pointed beams

My burning planet streams,

What rays were erst, in lightnings changed be:

When oft I muse, how I to those extremes

1. *clips* embraces   2. *hap* fortune   3. *lapped* enfolded

Am brought, I find no cause, except that she
In Love's bright zodiac having traced each room,
To fatal Sirius now at last is come.   4

Amaryllis to her dog Perlin

Fair Perlin do not bark!
Poor fool, dost thou not know
My lover, my desire?
If thou dost turn my foe,
Who to me shall be true?
Thou near shall after any kisses have.
Is't not enough all day
That thou do with me stay?
Give place to night and, like her, silent be,
Lulled with the noise that kisses make to thee.

4. *Sirius* Dog Star (associated with madness)

ROBERT HERRICK
(bap. 1591, d. 1674)

HERRICK WAS A clergyman with royalist sympathies, who lived through the English Civil War. He was presented to the vicarage of Dean Prior on the edge of Dartmoor in 1629. He was an animal lover, with a pet sparrow called Phil; a black Berkshire pig called Gyp, whom he would take out for long walks, and who would follow him into other peoples' drawing-rooms; and a spaniel called Tracie, whom he mentions in one of his poems: "A Tracie I do keep, whereby I please / The more my rural privacy." It is appropriate that an admirer of Charles I should have kept a spaniel, to whom he wrote a moving epitaph.

Upon his Spaniel Tracie

Now thou art dead, no eye shall ever see,
For shape and service, spaniel like to thee.
This shall my love do, give thy sad death one
Tear, that deserves of me a million.

KATHERINE PHILIPS
(1631–1664)

THE DOG COMMEMORATED in Philips's poem is the breed known today as an Irish wolfhound, which is what her friend Lord Orrery owned.

The Irish Greyhound

Behold this creature's form and state,
Which nature therefore did create;
That to the world might be expressed
What mien there can be in a beast;
And that we in this shape may find
A lion of another kind;
For this heroic beast does seem
In majesty to rival him—
And yet vouchsafes, to man, to show
Both service and submission too.
From whence we this distinction have,
That beast is fierce, but this is brave.
This dog hath so himself subdued

That hunger cannot make him rude, 1
And his behaviour does confess 2
True courage dwells with gentleness:
With sternest wolves he dares engage
And acts on them successful rage;
Yet too much courtesy may chance
To put him out of countenance.
When in his opposers' blood
Fortune hath made his virtue good,
This creature from an act so brave
Grows not more sullen, but more grave;
Man's guard he would be, not his sport,
Believing he hath ventured for't;
But yet no blood or shed or spent
Can ever make him insolent.
    Few men of him to do great things have learned,
    And when they are done, to be so unconcerned.

1. ***rude*** unreasoning   2. ***confess*** reveal

ANNE FINCH, COUNTESS OF WINCHILSEA
(1661–1720)

THE CHIEF VIRTUE of Snarl the dog is his honesty: he tests the moral quality of those who cross his path, employing "An exquisite discerning by the scent." He can sniff out dishonesty, whether it be that of a flatterer, an insincere wit, a parasite, or a legalistic cheat.

The Dog and His Master

No better dog e'er kept his master's door
Than honest Snarl, who spared nor rich nor poor,
But gave the alarm when anyone drew nigh,
Nor let pretended friends pass fearless by:
For which reproved, as better fed than taught,
He rightly thus expostulates the fault.

To keep the house from rascals was my charge;
The task was great, and the commission large.
Nor did your worship e'er declare your mind,
That to the begging crew it was confined;
Who shrink an arm, or prop an able knee,
Or turn up eyes, till they're not seen, nor see.

To thieves, who know the penalty of stealth,
And fairly stake their necks against your wealth,
These are the known delinquents of the times,
And whips and Tyburn testify their crimes.
But since to me there was by nature lent
An exquisite discerning by the scent;
I trace a flatterer, when he fawns and leers,
A rallying wit, when he commends and jeers:
The greedy parasite I grudging note
Who praises the good bits that oil his throat;
I mark the lady you so fondly toast,
That plays your gold when all her own is lost;
The knave, who fences your estate by law,
Yet still reserves an undermining flaw.
These and a thousand more which I could tell
Provoke my growling and offend my smell.

JONATHAN SWIFT
(1667–1745)

SWIFT WAS SURROUNDED by street-dogs in Dublin and must have seen them constantly. Rebecca Dingley was one of his closest friends in Ireland and the companion of his beloved Stella (real name Esther Johnson). Mrs Dingley's lapdog, Tiger, was spoilt rotten, as is evident from another Swift poem, "Bec's Birthday," in which he describes her having "many an evening nap / With Tiger slabbering in her lap." The following epigram dates from 1726, but was not published until 1762.

On the Collar of Tiger, Mrs Dingley's Lapdog

Pray steal me not, I'm Mrs Dingley's,
Whose heart in this four-footed thing lies.

ALEXANDER POPE
(1688–1744)

Pope loved animals and wrote eloquently against their inhumane treatment, especially in the context of hunting. Throughout his life he was a breeder of Great Danes, all of whom he called Bounce. Pope gave one of Bounce's offspring to Frederick, Prince of Wales (1707–1751); an epigram Pope had engraved on the puppy's collar has become his most widely quoted poem. "Argus" reprises the episode from the *Odyssey* that begins this selection (see p. 19).

Epigram. Engraved on the Collar of a Dog which I gave to his Royal Highness

I am his Highness' dog at Kew;
Pray tell me sir, whose dog are you?

Argus

When wise Ulysses, from his native coast
Long kept by wars, and long by tempests tossed,
Arrived at last, poor, old, disguised, alone,
To all his friends, and even his Queen, unknown,
Changed as he was, with age, and toils, and cares,

Furrowed his reverend face, and white his hairs,
In his own palace forced to ask his bread,
Scorned by those slaves his former bounty fed,
Forgot of all his own domestic crew;
The faithful dog alone his rightful master knew!
Unfed, unhoused, neglected, on the clay,
Like an old servant now cashiered, he lay;
Touched with resentment of ungrateful man,
And longing to behold his ancient lord again.
Him when he saw—he rose, and crawled to meet,
('Twas all he could) and fawned, and licked his feet,
Seized with dumb joy—then falling by his side,
Owned his returning Lord, looked up, and died!

VINCENT BOURNE

(bap. 1694, d. 1747)

Translated by Charles Lamb

BOURNE, A LONDONER by birth, was a scholar at Cambridge and went on to become a schoolteacher at Westminster. Although he wrote only in Latin, his poetry collections were popular, reprinting until well into the nineteenth century. "Epitaph on a Dog," like a number of his other works, is inspired by his knowledge of metropolitan life. Dog-epitaphs began to be written in the early eighteenth century; the form would reach its apogee with Byron's "Inscription" for Boatswain (p. 110).

Epitaph on a Dog

Poor Irus' faithful wolf-dog here I lie
That wont to tend my old blind master's steps,
His guide and guard; nor, while my service lasted,
Had he occasion for that staff, with which
He now goes picking out his path in fear
Over the highways and crossings, but would plant,
Safe in the conduct of my friendly string,
A firm foot forward still, till he had reached

Dog-eared

His poor seat on some stone, nigh where the tide
Of passers-by in thickest confluence flowed,
To whom with loud and passionate laments
From morn to eve his dark estate he wailed—
Nor wailed to all in vain: some here and there,
The well-disposed and good, their pennies gave.
I meantime at his feet obsequious slept,
Not all asleep in sleep, but heart and ear
Pricked up at his least motion, to receive
At his kind hand my customary crumbs
And common portion in his feast of scraps;
Or when night warned us homeward, tired and spent
With our long day and tedious beggary.
        These were my manners, this my way of life,
Till age and slow disease me overtook,
And severed from my sightless master's side.
But lest the grace of so good deeds should die,
Through tract of years in mute oblivion lost,
This slender tomb of turf hath Irus reared,
Cheap monument of no ungrudging hand,
And with short verse inscribed it, to attest,
In long and lasting union to attest,
The virtues of the beggar and his dog.

OLIVER GOLDSMITH
(ca. 1728–1774)

GAMBLER, FLAUTIST, APOTHECARY, continental traveler, and writer, Goldsmith is one of the eighteenth century's more flamboyant characters. In *The Citizen of the World* (1762), he condemned cruelty to animals, particularly when inflicted to provide meat for the table. "An Elegy on the Death of a Mad Dog" was written at the height of a scare about the consequences of dog bites—but Goldsmith's sympathies are with the dog. The poem's final line has become resoundingly famous in the annals of literature.

An Elegy on the Death of a Mad Dog

Good people all of every sort,
    Give ear unto my song,
And if you find it wondrous short
    It cannot hold you long.

In Islington there was a man
    Of whom the world might say
That still a godly race he ran
    Whene'er he went to pray.

A kind and gentle heart he had
    To comfort friends and foes;
The naked every day he clad
    When he put on his clothes.

And in that town a dog was found,
    As many dogs there be,
Both mongrel, puppy, whelp and hound,
    And curs of low degree.

This dog and man at first were friends,
    But when a pique began,
The dog, to gain some private ends,
    Went mad and bit the man.

Around from all the neighboring streets
    The wondering neighbors ran,
And swore the dog had lost his wits
    To bite so good a man.

The wound it seemed both sore and sad
    To every Christian eye,
And while they swore the dog was mad,
    They swore the man would die.

But soon a wonder came to light
    That showed the rogues they lied:
The man recovered of the bite,
    The dog it was that died.

WILLIAM COWPER
(1731–1800)

COWPER (PRONOUNCED "COOPER") advocated the humane treatment of animals, not least in his autobiographical poem *The Task* (1784), which describes his taming of three hares—Puss, Tiney, and Bess. He also cared for a menagerie of birds, and was as devoted to his tortoiseshell cat as to his spaniel, Beau—the protagonist and respondent of this poem.

On a Spaniel Called Beau, Killing a Young Bird

A spaniel, Beau, that fares like you,
    Well-fed and at his ease,
Should wiser be than to pursue
    Each trifle that he sees.

But you have killed a tiny bird
    Which flew not till today,
Against my orders, whom you heard
    Forbidding you the prey.

Nor did you kill that you might eat
    And ease a doggish pain,

For him, though chased with furious heat,
    You left where he was slain.

Nor was he of the thievish sort
    Or one whom blood allures,
But innocent was all his sport
    Whom you have torn for yours.

My dog, what remedy remains
    Since, teach you all I can,
I see you, after all my pains,
    So much resemble man.

Beau's Reply
Sir, when I flew to seize the bird
    In spite of your command,
A louder voice than yours I heard
    And harder to withstand.

You cried, "Forbear!," but in my breast
    A mightier cried "Proceed!"
'Twas Nature, sir, whose strong behest
    Impelled me to the deed.

Yet much as Nature I respect,
    I ventured once to break
(As you perhaps may recollect)
    Her precept for your sake;

And when your linnet on a day,
    Passing his prison door,
Had fluttered all his strength away
    And panting pressed the floor,

Well knowing him a sacred thing
    Not destined to my tooth,
I only kissed his ruffled wing
    And licked the feathers smooth.

Let my obedience *then* excuse
    My disobedience *now*,
Nor some reproof yourself refuse
    From your aggrieved bow-wow;

If killing birds be such a crime
    (Which I can hardly see),
What think you, sir, of killing Time
    With verse addressed to me?

JOHN WOLCOT ("PETER PINDAR")
(bap. 1738, d. 1819)

DOCTOR, SOMETIME PRIEST, and rumbustious satirist under the name "Peter Pindar," Wolcot lived long enough to know Dr. Johnson, as well as the Romantic writers who came after him. Although Wolcot's favorite manner was satire, "The Old Shepherd's Dog" is a serious poem about the bond between man and beast. Wolcot didn't like cats, which he thought "mean and suspicious," but loved dogs: "But the Dog is my delight:—tread on *his* tail or foot, he expresses, for a moment, the uneasiness of his feelings; but in a moment the complaint is ended. He runs around you, jumps against you, seems to declare his sorrow for complaining, as it was not intentionally done, nay, to make himself the aggressor, and begs, by whinings and lickings, that Master will think of it no more."

The Old Shepherd's Dog

The old shepherd's dog, like his master, was grey,
His teeth all departed, and feeble his tongue;
Yet where'er Corin went, he was followed by Tray—
Thus happy through life did they hobble along.

When, fatigued, on the grass the shepherd would lie,
For a nap in the sun, midst his slumbers so sweet,
His faithful companion crawled constantly nigh,
Placed his head on his lap or lay down at his feet.

When winter was heard on the hill and the plain,
And torrents descended, and cold was the wind,
If Corin went forth mid the tempests and rain,
Tray scorned to be left in the chimney behind.

At length in the straw Tray made his last bed,
For vain, against death, is the stoutest endeavor—
To lick Corin's hand he reared up his weak head
Then fell back, closed his eyes, and, ah! closed them forever.

Not long after Tray did the shepherd remain,
Who oft o'er his grave with true sorrow would bend;
And, when dying, thus feebly was heard the poor swain,
"Oh bury me, neighbors, beside my old friend!"

HANNAH MORE
(1745–1833)

HANNAH MORE WAS one of the most famous writers of her day—and one of the wealthiest. (When she died, she left the sum of £30,000 to some seventy charities.) The number of dogs that appear in her work indicate her love for the canine world. One of her earliest poems was an ode addressed to the actor David Garrick's dog Dragon, who had appeared onstage at Drury Lane, to the great delight of the audience. Throughout More's life, she fought against animal cruelty; poems such as "Patient Joe" were fundamental to her effort to convince readers of the sacredness of the animal world.

Patient Joe, or The Newcastle Collier

Have you heard of a collier of honest renown,
Who dwelt on the borders of Newcastle town?
His name it was Joseph—you better may know
If I tell you he always was called Patient Joe.

Whatever betided, he thought it was right,
And Providence still he kept ever in sight;

To those who love God, let things turn as they would,
He was certain that all worked together for good.

He praised his Creator whatever befell;
How thankful was Joseph when matters went well!
How sincere were his carols of praise for good health,
And how grateful for any increase in his wealth.

In trouble he bowed him to God's holy will,
How contented was Joseph when matters went ill;
When rich and when poor, he alike understood
That all things together were working for good.

If the land was afflicted with war, he declared
'Twas a needful correction for sins which *he* shared;
And when merciful Heaven bade slaughter to cease,
How thankful was Joe for the blessing of peace.

When taxes ran high and provisions were dear,
Still Joseph declared he had nothing to fear;
It was but a trial he well understood,
From Him who made all work together for good.

Though his wife was but sickly, his gettings but small, ¹
Yet a mind so submissive prepared him for all;
He lived on his gains, were they greater or less,
And the Giver he ceased not each moment to bless.

1. *gettings* earnings

When another child came, he received him with joy,
And Providence blessed, who had sent him the boy;
But when the child died, said poor Joe, "I'm content,
For God had a right to recall what he lent."

It was Joseph's ill fortune to work in a pit
With some who believed that profaneness was wit;
When disasters befell him, much pleasure they showed,
And laughed, and said, "Joseph, will this work for good?"

But ever when these would profanely advance,
That *this* happened by luck, and *that* happened by chance,
Still Joseph insisted no chance could be found,
Not a sparrow by accident falls to the ground.

Among his companions who worked in the pit,
And made him the butt of their profligate wit,
Was idle Tim Jenkins, who drank and who gamed,
Who mocked at his Bible, and was not ashamed.

One day at the pit his old comrades he found,
And they chatted, preparing to go underground;
Tim Jenkins as usual was turning to jest
Joe's notion—that all things which happened were best.

As Joe on the ground had unthinkingly laid
His provision for dinner of bacon and bread,
A dog on the watch seized the bread and the meat,
And off with his prey ran with footsteps so fleet.

Now to see the delight that Tim Jenkins expressed!
"Is the loss of thy dinner too, Joe, for the best?"
"No doubt on't," said Joe, "but as I must eat,
'Tis my duty to try to recover my meat."

So saying, he followed the dog a long round,
While Tim, laughing and swearing, went down underground.
Poor Joe soon returned, though his bacon was lost,
For the dog a good dinner had made at his cost.

When Joseph came back, he expected a sneer,
But the face of each collier spoke horror and fear;
"What a narrow escape hast thou had!" they all said,
"The pit is fallen in, and Tim Jenkins is dead!"

How sincere was the gratitude Joseph expressed;
How warm the compassion which glowed in his breast.
Thus events great and small, if aright understood,
Will be found to be working together for good.

"When my meat," Joseph cried, "was just now stolen away,
And I had no prospect of eating today,
How could it appear to a short-sighted sinner
That my life would be saved by the loss of my dinner?"

HELEN MARIA WILLIAMS
(1762–1827)

ONE OF THE more courageous women of her time, Williams believed in the ideals of the French Revolution and lived in Paris throughout the upheaval, at considerable danger to herself. She believed animal rights should be included among Napoleon's reforms: "Had I any influence in the proposal or fabrication of laws, I should . . . form a code for the protection of animals. In this age of rights, can no one be found fantastically humane enough to make their wrongs a theme of public attention? . . . Can no law succor that wretched horse, worn to the bone from famine and fatigue, lashed by his cruel tyrant into exertion beyond his strength, while he drags, in some vile vehicle, six persons, besides his merciless owner?" When the family dog, Bibi, died in 1815, Williams had him stuffed and his heart preserved. "Perhaps you have not forgotten," she told her friend Ruth Barlow, "the extreme urbanity of his manners and the caresses he lavished on our friends." Among his various funeral honors was Williams's elegy, "Lines on the Tomb of a Favorite Dog."

Lines on the Tomb of a Favorite Dog

Here rests the image of a friend,
Thine, cherished Bibi, thine!
Oft to this spot our steps we'll bend,
And call it Friendship's shrine.

Through lengthening years' successive flight
Thy fondness still had power
To shed its narrow line of light
On life's domestic hour;

And while for pleasures sought amiss
Abroad we vainly roam,
How far more dear the slightest bliss
That adds one charm to home!

Let those who coldly scorn the tear
That soothes the grief we prove,
Say, if fidelity be dear,
If love has claims to love;

Say, on what hallowed spot there lives
A heart unknown to range,
That to one chosen object gives
A love no power can change?

Tell, in what tender breast to find
Affection half so true?
Ah, Bibi, who of humankind
Has learnt to love like you!

WILLIAM WORDSWORTH
(1770–1850)

BY THE TIME Wordsworth was writing, poets such as Hannah More and William Cowper had begun writing about dogs as beings endowed with a higher wisdom: Wordsworth saw that borne out on a daily basis as a boy growing up in the English Lake District, where intelligent sheepdogs still round up livestock and are treated as members of the family. "Fidelity" isn't about a sheepdog but a spaniel—specifically Foxie, who belonged to the artist Charles Gough (1784–1805). While hiking in the Lake District, Gough fell to his death from Striding Edge, a perilously narrow ridge of rock leading to the top of Helvellyn Mountain. Foxie guarded his corpse faithfully for three months until she could attract the attention of a passing shepherd. The incident was first turned into a poem by Walter Scott (see pp. 98–99), but Wordsworth's retelling is no less loved by readers. *The Prelude* is his autobiographical masterpiece; in one of its best passages, he recalls returning from university to the Lake District one summer, to be greeted by his favorite companion, "a rough terrier of the hills"— probably a border terrier of the kind now bred on both sides of the Atlantic. The dog helps him write poems by listening and by ensuring the poet's composing habits don't make people think him mad.

Fidelity

A barking sound the shepherd hears,
A cry as of a dog or fox;
He halts and searches with his eyes
Among the scattered rocks:
And now at distance can discern
A stirring in a brake of fern,
From which immediately leaps out
A dog, and yelping runs about.

The dog is not of mountain breed,
Its motions, too, are wild and shy,
With something, as the Shepherd thinks,
Unusual in its cry;
Nor is there anyone in sight
All round, in hollow or on height,
Nor shout, nor whistle strikes his ear—
What is the creature doing here?

It was a cove, a huge recess
That keeps till June December's snow;
A lofty precipice in front,
A silent tarn below.   1
Far in the bosom of Helvellyn   2

1. **tarn** mountain lake   2. **Helvellyn** mountain at the heart of the Lake District, 3,117 feet high

Remote from public road or dwelling,
Pathway or cultivated land,
From trace of human foot or hand.

There sometimes does a leaping fish
Send through the tarn a lonely cheer;
The crags repeat the raven's croak
In symphony austere;
Thither the rainbow comes, the cloud,
And mists that spread the flying shroud,
And sunbeams, and the sounding blast
That, if it could, would hurry past,
But that enormous barrier holds it fast.

Not knowing what to think, awhile
The shepherd stood, then makes his way
Towards the dog, o'er rocks and stones
As quickly as he may;
Nor far had gone before he found
A human skeleton on the ground,
Sad sight! the shepherd with a sigh
Looks round to learn the history.

From those abrupt and perilous rocks
The man had fallen, that place of fear!
At length upon the shepherd's mind
It breaks, and all is clear:
He instantly recalled the name,
And who he was, and whence he came;

Remembered, too, the very day
On which the traveler passed this way.

But hear a wonder now, for sake
Of which this mournful tale I tell!
A lasting monument of words
This wonder merits well.
The dog, which still was hovering nigh,
Repeating the same timid cry—
This dog had been through three months' space
A dweller in that savage place.

Yes, proof was plain that, since the day
When this ill-fated traveler died,
The dog had watched about the spot
Or by his master's side:
How nourished here through such long time
He knows who gave that love sublime,
And gave that strength of feeling—great
Above all human estimate.

Incident Characteristic of a Favourite Dog[3]

On his morning rounds the master
Goes to learn how all things fare;
Searches pasture after pasture,
Sheep and cattle eyes with care;
And, for silence or for talk,

3. Wordsworth later noted that the dog who is the subject of this poem—called
Music—belonged to his brother-in-law, Thomas Hutchinson.

He hath comrades in his walk:
Four dogs, each pair of different breed,
Distinguished two for scent, and two for speed.

See a hare before him started!
Off they fly in earnest chase;
Every dog is eager-hearted,
All the four are in the race:
And the hare whom they pursue
Knows from instinct what to do;
Her hope is near: no turn she makes;
But like an arrow, to the river takes.

Deep the river was, and crusted
Thinly by a one night's frost;
But the nimble hare hath trusted
To the ice, and safely crossed;
She hath crossed, and without heed
All are following at full speed,
When, lo! the ice, so thinly spread,
Breaks—and the greyhound, Dart, is overhead!   4

Better fate have Prince and Swallow—
See them cleaving to the sport!
Music has no heart to follow,
Little Music, she stops short.
She hath neither wish nor heart,

4. *overhead* submerged

Hers is now another part:
A loving creature she, and brave!
And fondly strives her struggling friend to save.

From the brink her paws she stretches,
Very hands as you would say!
And afflicting moans she fetches,
As he breaks the ice away.
For herself she hath no fears,
Him alone she sees and hears,
Makes efforts with complainings; nor gives o'er
Until her fellow sinks to reappear no more.

Tribute to the Memory of the Same Dog[5]

Lie here, without a record of thy worth,
Beneath a covering of the common earth!
It is not from unwillingness to praise,
Or want of love, that here no stone we raise;
More thou deserv'st; but *this* man gives to man,
Brother to brother, *this* is all we can.
Yet they to whom thy virtues made thee dear
Shall find thee through all changes of the year:
This oak points out thy grave; the silent tree
Will gladly stand a monument of thee.
We grieved for thee, and wished thy end were past;
And willingly have laid thee here at last:
For thou hadst lived till everything that cheers

5. Thomas Hutchinson's dog Music died, blind and old, when he fell into a well.

In thee had yielded to the weight of years;
Extreme old age had wasted thee away,
And left thee but a glimmering of the day;
Thy ears were deaf, and feeble were thy knees,
I saw thee stagger in the summer breeze,
Too weak to stand against its sportive breath,
And ready for the gentlest stroke of death.
It came, and we were glad; yet tears were shed;
Both man and woman wept when thou wert dead;
Not only for a thousand thoughts that were,
Old household thoughts, in which thou hadst thy share;
But for some precious boons vouchsafed to thee,
Found scarcely anywhere in like degree!
For love, that comes wherever life and sense
Are given by God, in thee was most intense;
A chain of heart, a feeling of the mind,
A tender sympathy, which did thee bind
Not only to us men, but to thy kind:
Yea, for thy fellow-brutes in thee we saw
A soul of love, love's intellectual law:
Hence, if we wept, it was not done in shame;
Our tears from passion and from reason came,
And therefore shalt thou be an honored name!

The Prelude, Book 4 (extract)

Among the faces which it pleased me well
To see again, was one by ancient right
Our inmate—a rough terrier of the hills,
By birth and call of Nature preordained

To hunt the badger, and unearth the fox
Among the impervious crags; but, having been
From youth our own adopted, he had passed
Into a gentler service. And when first
The boyish spirit flagged, and day by day
Along my veins I kindled with the stir,
The fermentation and the vernal heat
Of poesy, affecting private shades
Like a sick lover, then this dog was used
To watch me, an attendant and a friend
Obsequious to my steps, early and late,
Though often of such dilatory walk
Tired, and uneasy at the halts I made.
A hundred times when, in these wanderings,
I have been busy with the toil of verse,
Great pains and little progress, and at once
Some fair enchanting image in my mind
Rose up, full-formed, like Venus from the sea,
Have I sprung forth towards him, and let loose
My hand upon his back with stormy joy,
Caressing him again, and yet again.

      And when, in the public roads at eventide
I sauntered, like a river murmuring
And talking to itself, at such a season
It was his custom to jog on before;
But duly, whensoever he had met
A passenger approaching, would he turn
To give me timely notice, and straitway,

Punctual to such admonishment, I hushed
My voice, composed my gait, and shaped myself
To give and take a greeting that might save
My name from piteous rumors such as wait
On men suspected to be crazed in brain.

WALTER SCOTT
(1771–1832)

ON APRIL 17, 1805, the twenty-one-year-old artist Charles Gough, on a hiking expedition in the Lake District, was caught in a hailstorm as he crossed Striding Edge (a narrow ridge of rock leading to the summit of Helvellyn) and fell to his death. He was killed instantly. His dog Foxie guarded his body for several months, surviving on grass and snails, until she attracted the attention of a passing shepherd in the third week of July. By then Gough's body was a skeleton, and Foxie's fur had turned white because of exposure to the cold Lake District weather. (Local people were certain the body had been eaten by birds.) The incident would provide the basis for one of Scott's most successful short poems, "Helvellyn," published in 1806. Scott owned a succession of dogs throughout his life; apparently he enjoyed speaking to them, and assumed they could understand every word he said. He adored them all, especially Maida (named after the 1806 Battle of Maida), a cross between a Scottish greyhound and a Pyrenean sheepdog, given to Scott by the Highland chief Glengarry. Maida was painted by William Allan and Alexander Nasmyth, and is depicted in the Scott Monument in Edinburgh. Another dog, Camp, a bull terrier, was painted by Henry Raeburn.

Helvellyn

In the spring of 1805, a young gentleman of talents, and of a most amiable disposition, perished by losing his way on the mountain Helvellyn. His remains were not discovered till three months afterwards, when they were found guarded by a faithful terrier, his constant attendant during frequent solitary rambles through the wilds of Cumberland and Westmoreland.

I climbed the dark brow of the mighty Helvellyn,
　　Lakes and mountains beneath me gleamed misty and wide:
All was still save, by fits, when the eagle was yelling,
　　And starting around me the echoes replied.
On the right, Striden Edge round the Red Tarn was bending,
And Catchedicam its left verge was defending,　　　　　　　　　　1
One huge nameless rock in the front was ascending,
　　When I marked the sad spot where the wanderer had died.
Dark green was that spot mid the brown mountain heather,
　　Where the pilgrim of nature lay stretched in decay.
Like the corpse of an outcast abandoned to weather,
　　Till the mountain winds wasted the tenantless clay;
Not yet quite deserted, though lonely extended,
For faithful in death, his mute favorite attended,
The much-loved remains of her master defended,
　　And chased the hill-fox and the raven away.

1. *Catchedicam*: Scott refers to the mountain today known as Catstye Cam, nearly three thousand feet high, to the immediate northeast of Helvellyn. The southerly spur of Helvellyn is Striding Edge. Red Tarn (a lake up in the mountains) is to the east of Helvellyn's summit.

How long didst thou think that his silence was slumber?
　　When the wind waved his garment, how oft didst thou start?
How many long days and long nights didst thou number
　　Ere he faded before thee, the friend of thy heart?
And oh, was it meet that—no requiem read o'er him,
No mother to weep, and no friend to deplore him,
And thou, little guardian, alone stretched before him—
　　Unhonored the pilgrim from life should depart?
When a prince to the fate of the peasant has yielded,
　　The tapestry waves dark round the dim-lighted hall,
With scutcheons of silver the coffin is shielded,
　　And pages stand mute by the canopied pall;
Through the courts, at deep midnight, the torches are gleaming;
In the proudly arched chapel the banners are beaming;
Far adown the long aisle sacred music is streaming,
　　Lamenting a chief of the people should fall.
But meeter for thee, gentle lover of nature,
　　To lay down thy head like the meek mountain lamb,
When, wildered, he drops from some cliff huge in stature,
　　And draws his last sob by the side of his dam.
And more stately thy couch by this desert lake lying,
Thy obsequies sung by the gray plover flying,
With one faithful friend but to witness thy dying,
　　In the arms of Helvellyn and Catchedicam.

SAMUEL TAYLOR COLERIDGE
(1772–1834)

"THE ONE ABSOLUTELY unselfish friend that man can have in this selfish world, the one that never deserts him, the one that never proves ungrateful or treacherous, is his dog." That remark, from Coleridge's *Table Talk*, testifies to his high regard for dogs, but I have no evidence he ever owned one. The most famous dog in his poetry—and among the best known in literature—has to be the "mastiff bitch" in *Christabel*, a moral touchstone whose ability to sniff out evil deserves to be trusted.

Outside her kennel, the mastiff old
Lay fast asleep in moonshine cold.
The mastiff old did not awake,
Yet she an angry moan did make.
And what can ail the mastiff bitch?
Never till now she uttered yell
Beneath the eye of Christabel.
Perhaps it is the owlet's scritch,
For what can ail the mastiff bitch? (Part 1.ll.145–153)

The mastiff's unheeded warnings lead one to believe that Christabel might be the author of her own destruction. Coleridge also wrote the epigram "For a House-Dog's Collar," in 1802, a translation of Martin Opitz, a German author.

For a House-Dog's Collar (from Opitz)

When thieves come, I bark; when gallants, I am still—
So perform both my master's and my mistress's will.

THOMAS CAMPBELL
(1777–1844)

Campbell, a Glaswegian by birth, became a celebrated poet with the appearance of *The Pleasures of Hope* in 1799; it included "The Harper."

The Harper

On the green banks of Shannon, when Sheelah was nigh,
No blithe Irish lad was so happy as I;
No harp like my own could so cheerily play,
And wherever I went was my poor dog Tray.

When at last I was forced from my Sheelah to part,
She said (while the sorrow was big at her heart),
"Oh remember your Sheelah when far far away
And be kind, my dear Pat, to our poor dog Tray."

Poor dog, he was faithful and kind, to be sure,
And he constantly loved me, although I was poor;
When the sour-looking folk sent me heartless away,
I had always a friend in my poor dog Tray.

Dog-eared

When the road was so dark, and the night was so cold,
And Pat and his dog were grown weary and old,
How snugly we slept in my old coat of gray,
And he licked me for kindness, my poor dog Tray.

Though my wallet was scant, I remembered his case,
Nor refused my last crust to his pitiful face;
But he died at my feet on a cold winter day,
And I played a sad lament for my poor dog Tray.

Where now shall I go—poor, forsaken and blind?
Can I find one to guide me, so faithful and kind?
To my sweet native village, so far far away,
I can never more return with my poor dog Tray.

SYDNEY OWENSON, LADY MORGAN
(bap. 1783, d. 1859)

BEST KNOWN TO contemporaries as a novelist and travel writer, Owenson was also a poet. In this elegy she laments Bell, a lapdog who died at the age of seven.

On the Death of a Favorite Lapdog

Since then thy life's "poor play is o'er,"
And thou canst live to charm no more,
    Who charmed so well;
Let me whose hours you oft beguiled,
Who at thy sportive ways oft smiled,
    Thy virtues tell!

Though courted, followed, and admired,
Yet you no flattering praise desired,
    But loved to shun
The crowd, and chose an humble lot,
And chastely, unobtrusive, not
    "Unsought be won."

Thy sex's faults to thee unknown,
To gadding nor to flirting prone,
    Thou ne'er wert seen;
With smiles invidious to disgrace,
The mild expression of thy face,
    By envious spleen!

Nor with a foul, malicious tongue,
To do thy friend or neighbor wrong;
    But ever ready
With all thy power to defend
Thy neighbor, or thy much-loved friend,
    With courage steady!

Possessed of many a wily charm,
The heart of sorrow to disarm,
    You constant proved;
For seven long years with sportive play,
To chase dull thought and care away,
    From those you loved!

Nor female like, didst thou e'er pant
For dress, or showy baubles want;
    And didst desire
But cleanliness devoid of art,
Pure emblem of thy purer heart,
    Thy best attire.

With brilliant eyes of jetty dye,
And teeth that did with ivory vie,
    And skin of snow;
With loveliness of form blest,
Yet that those charms you e'er possessed,
    You ne'er did know!

Cosmetic aid you'd ne'er implore,
A faded charm to restore,
    Or age repel;
Yet may I say with friendly pride,
That charms were thine, and that you died,
    And lived a Bell.

GEORGE GORDON, LORD BYRON
(1788–1824)

'Tis sweet to hear the watchdog's honest bark
    Bay deep-mouthed welcome as we draw near home;
'Tis sweet to know there is an eye will mark
    Our coming, and look brighter when we come.
  (*Don Juan*, Canto 1)

WERE THIS ALL we had to go on, it would be enough to reveal Byron's love of dogs. Boatswain (pronounced "Bosun"), the New-foundland, was acquired when Byron was fifteen. After the dog caught rabies, Byron nursed him fearlessly until Boatswain died. Grief-stricken, Byron wrote an epitaph, later carved onto an elaborate tomb erected at his ancestral home, Newstead Abbey; it remains one of the most impressive to the memory of a dog. Byron's friend John Cam Hobhouse wrote an explanation: "Near this spot are deposited the remains of one who possessed beauty without vanity, strength without insolence, courage without ferocity, and all the virtues of man without his vices. This praise, which would be unmeaning flattery if inscribed over human ashes, is but a just tribute to the memory of Boatswain, a dog who was born in Newfoundland, May 1803, and died at Newstead, November 18th, 1808." The text below is the earliest available, taken from Byron's fair copy; it is published here for the first time, and I am grateful to Professor Paul F. Betz for permission to use it.

Byron was an animal lover and owned a sizeable menagerie. When Percy Bysshe Shelley visited him in 1821, he found Byron living with "ten horses, eight enormous dogs, three monkeys, five cats, an eagle, a crow, and a falcon . . . five peacocks, two guinea hens, and an Egyptian crane," all of which (apart from the horses) were free to range as they wished round the house. As an undergraduate at Cambridge, Byron kept a bear in his rooms, dogs being prohibited, and there were reports of him being seen hugging the bear "with *fraternal* affection!"

Inscription on the Monument of a Newfoundland Dog

When some proud son of man returns to earth,
Unknown to glory, but upheld by birth,
The sculptor's art exhausts the pomp of woe,
And storied urns record who rests below;
When all is done, upon the tomb is seen
Not what he was, but what he should have been;
But the poor dog, in life the firmest friend,
The first to welcome, foremost to defend,
Whose honest heart is still his master's own,
Who labors, fights, lives, breathes, for him alone,
Unhonored falls, unnoticed all his worth,

Denied in heaven the soul he held on earth:
While man, vain insect! hopes to be forgiven,
And claims himself a sole exclusive heaven,
Oh man! thou feeble tenant of an hour,
Debased by slavery, or corrupt by power—
Who knows thee well must quit thee with disgust,
Degraded mass of animated dust!
Thy love is lust, thy friendship all a cheat,
Thy smiles hypocrisy, thy words deceit!
By nature vile, ennobled but by name,
Each kindred brute might bid thee blush for shame.
Ye, who perchance behold this simple urn,
Pass on—it honors none you wish to mourn;
To mark a friend's remains these stones arise;
I had but one, and here he lies. (Newstead Abbey, Oct. 30, 1808)

JOHN CLARE
(1793–1864)

CLARE WAS A farm laborer first, poet second—yet he has come to be regarded as one of the finest poets of his time. "On a Lost Greyhound" reveals an acute sensitivity to the natural world, as well as the close bond between country people and the animals around them.

On a Lost Greyhound Lying on the Snow

Ah, thou poor neglected hound!
    Now thou'st done with catching hares,
Thou may'st lie upon the ground
    Lost, for what thy master cares.
To see thee lie, it makes me sigh,
    A proud, hard-hearted man!
But men, we know, like dogs may go,
    When they've done all they can.

And thus, from witnessing thy fate,
    Thoughtful reflection wakes;
Though thou'rt a dog (with grief I say't),
    Poor man thy fare partakes:

Like thee, lost whelp, the poor man's help
  Erewhile so much desired,
Now harvest's got, is wanted not
  Or little is required.

So now the overplus will be,
  As useless negroes, all
Turned in the bitter blast like thee—
  Mere cumber-grounds, to fall;   1
But this reward, for toil so hard
  Is sure to meet return
From Him whose ear is always near
  When the oppressed mourn.

For dogs, as men, are equally
  A link in nature's chain,
Formed by the hand that formed me,
  Which formeth naught in vain;
All life contains, as 'twere by chains,
  From Him still perfect are,
Nor does He think the meanest link
  Unworthy of His care.

So let us both on Him rely,
  And He'll for us provide,
Find us a shelter warm and dry
  With everything beside;

1. ***cumber-grounds*** useless, unhelpful people

And while fools void of sense deride
    My tenderness to thee,
I'll take thee home from whence I've come—
    So rise and gang with me!   2

Poor patient thing, he seems to hear
    And know what I have said;
He wags his tail and ventures near,
    And bows his mournful head.
Thou'rt welcome, come! and though thou'rt dumb,
    Thy silence tells thy pains,
So with me start, to share a part,
    While I have aught remains.

2. *gang* go

WILLIAM BARNES
(1801–1886)

BARNES WAS A great dog lover. When he started to get ready for a walk, his dog, Cara, would begin dancing round the room, knowing that he would take her with him; she is the subject of "I and the dog." Barnes once remarked, "Why do we sometimes call a worthless fellow a dog? The fidelity, long-suffering, and love of dogs is so great that we cannot give the name to a false friend without doing him too much honour."

I and the dog

As I was wont to straggle out
To your house, oh! how glad the dog,
With low-put nose, would nimbly jog,
Along my path and hunt about;
And his great pleasure was to run
By timbered hedge and banky ledge,
And ended where my own begun,
At your old door and stonen floor.   1

---

1. **stonen** i.e., made of stone

And there, as time was gliding by,
With me so quick, with him so slow,
How he would look at me, and blow,
From time to time, a whining sigh,
That meant, "Now come along the land,
With timbered knolls, and rabbit holes,
I can't think what you have on hand,
With this young face, in this old place."

VICTOR HUGO
(1802–1885)
Translated by Duncan Wu

HUGO IS KNOWN to us mainly for his fiction—*The Hunchback of Notre-Dame* (1831) and *Les Misérables* (1862)—but he was also an accomplished poet. When he went into exile at St. Helier, Jersey, in 1852, he made friends with Ponto, a black spaniel who accompanied him on walks—the subject of the first of the poems here. Hugo remained there until 1855; he then moved to Guernsey, where he owned three dogs: Chougna, Lux, and Sénat (a greyhound). For Sénat he wrote a couplet, which he attached to the dog's collar:

I wish that someone would take me home.
Profession: dog. Master: Hugo. Name: Sénat.

The poems here are indicative of his love for dogs, who he believed had souls, were immortal, and could perceive God. In "Ponto," the spaniel confirms Hugo's moral reflections on the animal and human worlds.

Ponto

"Ponto, let's go!", to my black dog I cry,
And through woods, dressed as a peasant, stride;
I walk through vast woods, reading old books.
In winter, when branches make frosty networks,
Or summer, when all laugh, even weeping morn,
And flowers in triumph cover the lawn,
I take Froissart, Montluc, Tacitus, some story,
And march on, moved by crimes of glory—
Alas, horror all round, even the best:
Men in darkness betrayed by the rest,
The hands of the great, alas, blood-soiled;
Alexander drunk and mad, Caesar orgy-embroiled,
And Charlemagne—fist on Didier, foot on Widukind—   1
With Charles the Fifth too often akin;   2
With Cato feeding eels those slaves who've failed him;   3
Titus crucifying Jerusalem;   4
Turenne, heroic as Bayard and Catinat,   5

1. In 757, Duke Desiderius of Tuscany became King of the Lombards; he and Widukind, leader of the Saxons, were antagonists of Charlemagne.   2. Hugo compares Charlemagne (742–814) with the Holy Roman Emperor, Charles V (1500–1558), not to be confused with Charles V of France (1338–1380). 3. Although it would be reasonable to think that Hugo's reference to "Caton" is to Dionysius Cato, the more likely figure is Vedius Pollion (d. 15 BC), a Roman businessman who wanted to feed one of his slaves to a moray eel; the story is recounted by Seneca in *On Clemency*.   4. The Roman Emperor Titus (AD 39–81) besieged and entered Jerusalem in 70.   5. Hugo refers to Henri de La Tour d'Auvergne, vicomte de Turenne (1611–75); Pierre Terrail, seigneur de Bayard (1473–1524); and Nicolas Catinat (1637–1712), military commanders.

At Nördlingen, gangster of the Palatinate;　　　　　　6
The duels of Jarnac, and Carrouges; Louis the Ninth　　7
Slicing tongues and lips with a red-hot knife;　　　　8
Cromwell deceiving Milton, Calvin putting　　　　　　9
Servetus to the stake. Such are the ghosts scudding　　10
Round your bedside, oh Glory! I flee to nature,
And as I remark, "All is deceit, imposture,
Lies, iniquity, evil attired as merit",
Ponto follows. The dog's a good spirit
Which, unable to be man, becomes beast.
Ponto looks at me: honesty unleashed.
(*Marine-Terrace, March 3, 1855.*)

Un groupe tout à l'heure était là sur la grève (from *La Destinée*)

They stood just now on the sand by the sea,
Fixated by something: a dog lying
On the ground. "It's sick," the children said to me
As I reached them, "That's all this is. It's dying."

6. Turenne's army defeated the Bavarians at Allerheim near Nördlingen in August 1645. Turenne became master of the Palatinate in June 1674.　7. Hugo refers to the judicially ordered combats of Jarnac and Châtaigneraye in 1547, and of Jean de Carrouges IV and Jacques le Gris in 1386.　8. Louis IX (1214–70) introduced a strict punishment for blasphemy: mutilation of tongue and lips.　9. In his *History of the Commonwealth*, William Godwin argued that Cromwell deceived Milton.　10. Michael Servetus (1509–53) was a theologian burnt at the stake for heresy, thanks to the denunciations of Calvin.

The ocean rolled in, hurling foam at him.
"It's been like this for the last three days,"
Said the women, "it won't move a limb.
Speak, and it won't even open its eyes."

"His owner is at sea, he's a sailor,"
Said one old lady. Sticking his head out
Of a bay window, an old navigator
Called across the sands, "He's pining about

His owner—and see over there? The bark is
Just weighing anchor, he's returning now,
But his dog will have departed before his
Arrival." With how sad steps and slow

I shifted closer to the sad wet thing
That, deaf to this chatter, moved neither head
Nor body, eyes firmly shut, appearing
Inert on the ground. And as the pale red

Sun sank and evening descended, we could
See the owner hastening towards us, pace
Slowed by the pains of old age, as he murmured
Under his breath, in a very low voice,

The dog's name. Exhausted, the creature spied
Him; eyes full of shadows, he greeted him,
Wagging his old tail one last time—then died.
It was the hour when, as daylight goes dim,

The evening star seems like a flaming
Torch in the darkness, a pinprick of light
In the sky. And I couldn't help saying,
"Whence comes that star? Whither that dog? O Night!"
   (July 12, 1855)

ELIZABETH BARRETT BROWNING
(1806–1861)

THOUGH NOW REFERRED to as Elizabeth Barrett Browning (EBB), she referred to herself as Elizabeth Barrett Moulton Barrett, and later as Elizabeth Barrett Barrett. The gift to her of a spaniel from her friend Mary Russell Mitford marked the beginning of one of the greatest love stories of the Romantic period. EBB believed Flush to be of exceptional intelligence and taught him the alphabet so he could play board games with her. She fed him cakes, "feast-day macaroons," and large pieces of bread thickly buttered, and when the doctor disapproved of Flush's place on the sofa with EBB, she ensured he was hosed down daily. Flush was notoriously possessive of his mistress to the point of biting Robert Browning when he started to pay court to her; he bit him again several weeks later. Flush was dognapped no less than three times, and on each occasion EBB ensured the ransom was paid. In September 1846, she made the decision secretly to marry Browning against the wishes of her family. She stole away from the family house at 50 Wimpole Street in London and embarked for the continent, taking Flush with her. Flush made friends with Browning, and lived a happy life in Italy until his death in Florence in 1854. He is buried in the vaults of Casa Guidi, though no one knows precisely where.

Many years later, Flush was to become the protagonist of one of Virginia Woolf's most successful novels, *Flush: A Biography*.

To Flush, My Dog

Loving friend, the gift of one
Who her own true faith has run
    Through thy lower nature,
Be my benediction said
With my hand upon thy head,
    Gentle fellow-creature!

Like a lady's ringlets brown,
Flow thy silken ears adown
    Either side demurely
Of thy silver-suited breast,
Shining out from all the rest
    Of thy body purely.

Darkly brown thy body is,
Till the sunshine striking this
    Alchemize its dullness,
When the sleek curls manifold
Flash all over into gold
    With a burnished fullness.

Underneath my stroking hand,
Startled eyes of hazel bland
    Kindling, growing larger,

Up thou leapest with a spring,
Full of prank and curvetting,
    Leaping like a charger.

Leap! thy broad tail waves a light,
Leap! thy slender feet are bright,
    Canopied in fringes;
Leap! those tasseled ears of thine
Flicker strangely, fair and fine
    Down their golden inches.

Yet, my pretty, sportive friend,
Little is't to such an end
    That I praise thy rareness;
Other dogs may be thy peers
Haply in these drooping ears
    And this glossy fairness.

But of thee it shall be said,
This dog watched beside a bed
    Day and night unweary,
Watched within a curtained room
Where no sunbeam broke the gloom
    Round the sick and dreary.

Roses, gathered for a vase,
In that chamber died apace,
    Beam and breeze resigning;

This dog only, waited on,
Knowing that when light is gone
    Love remains for shining.

Other dogs in thymy dew
Tracked the hares and followed through
    Sunny moor or meadow;
This dog only crept and crept
Next a languid cheek that slept,
    Sharing in the shadow.

Other dogs of loyal cheer
Bounded at the whistle clear,
    Up the woodside hieing;
This dog only watched in reach
Of a faintly uttered speech
    Or a louder sighing.

And if one or two quick tears
Dropped upon his glossy ears
    Or a sigh came double,
Up he sprang in eager haste,
Fawning, fondling, breathing fast,
    In a tender trouble.

And this dog was satisfied
If a pale thin hand would glide
    Down his dewlaps sloping,

Which he pushed his nose within,
After platforming his chin
    On the palm left open.

This dog, if a friendly voice
Call him now to blither choice
    Than such chamber-keeping,
"Come out!" praying from the door,
Presseth backward as before,
    Up against me leaping.

Therefore to this dog will I,
Tenderly not scornfully,
    Render praise and favor:
With my hand upon his head,
Is my benediction said
    Therefore and forever.

And because he loves me so,
Better than his kind will do
    Often man or woman,
Give I back more love again
Than dogs often take of men,
    Leaning from my human.

Blessings on thee, dog of mine,
Pretty collars make thee fine,
    Sugared milk make fat thee!

Pleasures wag on in thy tail,
Hands of gentle motion fail
    Nevermore, to pat thee!

Downy pillow take thy head,
Silken coverlid bestead,
    Sunshine help thy sleeping!
No fly's buzzing wake thee up,
No man break thy purple cup
    Set for drinking deep in.

Whiskered cats arointed flee,   1
Sturdy stoppers keep from thee
    Cologne distillations;
Nuts lie in thy path for stones,
And thy feast-day macaroons
    Turn to daily rations!

Mock I thee, in wishing weal?
Tears are in my eyes to feel
    Thou art made so straitly,   2
Blessing needs must straiten too,
Little canst thou joy or do,
    Thou who lovest greatly.

1. *arointed* driven away   2. *straitly* thinly, i.e., with so little food

Yet be blessed to the height
Of all good and all delight
    Pervious to thy nature;
Only loved beyond that line,
With a love that answers thine,
    Loving fellow-creature!

Flush or Faunus

You see this dog; it was but yesterday
I mused forgetful of his presence here,
Till thought on thought drew downward tear on tear,
When from the pillow where wet-cheeked I lay,
A head as hairy as Faunus thrust its way
Right sudden against my face, two golden-clear
Great eyes astonished mine, a drooping ear
Did flap me on either cheek to dry the spray!
I started first as some Arcadian
Amazed by goatly god in twilight grove:
But, as the bearded vision closelier ran
My tears off, I knew Flush, and rose above
Surprise and sadness, thanking the true Pan
Who by low creatures leads to heights of love.

ROBERT BROWNING
(1812–1889)

BROWNING MAY NOT have realized, when he secretly married Elizabeth Barrett in September 1846, he was also marrying her dog: she was not prepared to leave Flush the spaniel at her family's house in London, and he eloped to the continent with both of them. Browning didn't mind: he had grown up with a pet bulldog. As an adult he loved animals of all kinds. On one occasion, he found a wounded goose in central London and took it home and nursed it to health. "I despise and abhor the pleas on behalf of that infamous practice, vivisection," he wrote, "I would rather submit to the worst of deaths, so far as pain goes, than have a single dog or cat tortured to death on the pretense of sparing me a twinge or two." In later years he became vice president of the Victoria Street Society (VSS), founded in 1875, a year before Parliament made vivisection legal, thus guaranteeing secrecy to its practitioners. The VSS changed its name in 1897 to the National Anti-Vivisection Society and continues its work to this day. "Tray" is a kind of horror story; it is Browning's attempt to persuade readers of the injustice of vivisection, and to ridicule the idea that it was possible to discover an animal's soul by slicing open its brain. One of

Browning's friends did actually witness a dog saving a child's life in Paris, as described in the following poem.

Tray

Sing me a hero! Quench my thirst
Of soul, ye bards!
                         Quoth Bard the first:
"Sir Olaf, the good knight, did don
His helm and eke his habergeon . . ."
Sir Olaf and his bard!

"That sin-scathed brow," quoth Bard the second,
"That eye wide ope as though Fate beckoned
My hero to some steep, beneath
Which precipice smiled tempting death
You too without your host have reckoned!"

 "A beggar-child"—let's hear this third!
"Sat on a quay's edge; like a bird
Sang to herself at careless play
And fell into the stream. 'Dismay!
Help, you the standers-by!' None stirred.

Bystanders reason, think of wives
And children ere they risk their lives.
Over the balustrade has bounced
A mere instinctive dog, and pounced
Plumb on the prize. 'How well he dives!

Up he comes with the child, see, tight
In mouth, alive too, clutched from quite
A depth of ten feet—twelve, I bet!
Good dog! What, off again? There's yet
Another child to save? All right!

How strange we saw no other fall!
It's instinct in the animal.
Good dog! But he's a long while under:
If he got drowned I should not wonder—
Strong current, that against the wall!

Here he comes, holds in mouth this time—
What may the thing be? Well, that's prime!
Now, did you ever? Reason reigns
In man alone, since all Tray's pains
Have fished—the child's doll from the slime!'

And so, amid the laughter gay,
Trotted my hero off, old Tray,
Till somebody, prerogatived   1
With reason, reasoned: 'Why he dived,
His brain would show us, I should say.

John, go and catch—or, if needs be,
Purchase—that animal for me!

1. *prerogatived* endowed, gifted (ironic)

By vivisection, at expense
Of half-an-hour and eighteenpence,
How brain secretes dog's soul, we'll see!'"

IVAN TURGENEV

(1818–1883)

Translated by Constance Garnett

TURGENEV IS THE author of what has been described as the greatest dog story in Russian literature, "Mumu," which describes how Gerasim, a deaf and dumb man, saves a dog from drowning. Turgenev also wrote a short story in 1866, in which a character is prompted to acquire a dog by a ghost under his bed. Neither qualifies for admission here, but the prose work below was written as a poem and is therefore included. Turgenev took the idea of the prose-poem from Charles Baudelaire; when he wrote the piece, he was resident in Paris, where he could easily obtain *Paris Spleen* (1869), in which he read "The Good Dogs" (p. 144).

The Dog

Us two in the room; my dog and me. . . . Outside a fearful storm is howling. The dog sits in front of me, and looks me straight in the face. And I, too, look into his face. He wants, it seems, to tell me something. He is dumb, he is without words, he does not understand himself—but I understand him.

I understand that at this instant there is living in him and in me the same feeling, that there is no difference between us. We are the same; in each of us there burns and shines the same trembling spark.

Death sweeps down, with a wave of its chill broad wing. . . . And the end!

Who then can discern what was the spark that glowed in each of us? No! We are not beast and man that glance at one another. . . . They are the eyes of equals, those eyes riveted on one another. And in each of these, in the beast and in the man, the same life huddles up in fear close to the other. (February 1878)

JOHN RUSKIN
(1819–1900)

As a FIVE-YEAR-OLD, Ruskin was attacked by a black Newfoundland called Lion, who bit off part of his upper lip. It didn't hinder his love of dogs, and he later recalled that his aunt's dog Towzer, who guarded her bakery, was "my chief companion"—"a vulgar dog, though a very good and dear dog." Ruskin made a point of getting to know dogs of friends and acquaintances, and in the course of a long life enjoyed the company of his own bulldogs, St. Bernards, and collies. He inherited Dash, a brown-and-white King Charles, from his aunt when she died. "The Summit" included below comes from Ruskin's poem-sequence, "A Tour of the Continent," and reprises the story of Charles Gough, familiar from poems by Walter Scott and William Wordsworth (see pp. 87–90, 98–99).

My Dog Dash

I have a dog of Blenheim birth,
With fine long ears, and full of mirth;
And sometimes, running o'er the plain,
    He tumbles on his nose:
But quickly jumping up again,
    Like lightning on he goes!

'Tis queer to watch his gambols gay;
He's very loving—in his way:
He even wants to lick your face,
But that is somewhat out of place.
'Tis well enough your hand to kiss;
But Dash is not content with this!
Howe'er, let all his faults be past,
I'll praise him to the very last.
His love is true, though somewhat violent,
With truth I say he's seldom silent;
If any man approach the gate
A bow-wow-wow rings through his pate—
Attempts to quiet Dash are vain
Till clear of all is his domain.

The Summit

Oh, we are on the mountain-top!
The clouds float by in fleecy flock,
Heavy, and dank. Around, below,
A wilderness of turf and snow—
Scanty rock-turf or marble bare
Without a living thing; for there
Not a bird clove the thin, cold air
With laboring wing: the very goat
To such a height ascendeth not,
And if the cloud's thick drapery
Clove for a moment, you would see
The long white snow-fields on each side
Clasping the mountain-breast, or heaped

In high, wreathed hills whence torrents leaped,
And gathering force, as down they well
To aid the swift Rhine's headlong swell.
And here and there a moldering cross
Of dark pine, matted o'er with moss,
Hung on the precipice to tell
Where some benighted traveler fell;
Or where the avalanche's leap
Hurled down, with its wild thunder-sweep,
Him unexpecting; and to pray
The passing traveler to stay,
And, looking from the precipice
Dizzily down to the abyss,
To wing to heaven one short prayer—
One, for the soul that parted there.
    I thought, as by the cross I passed,
Of far Helvellyn's dreary waste,
Mid my own hills, and legend strange;
How from dark Striden's ridgy range
One fell, upon a wintry day
When snow wreaths white concealed his way,
And died beside a small dark tarn
O'erlooked by crags, whose foreheads stern
Shut in a little vale—a spot
By men unknown and trodden not—
Green, and most beautiful, and lay
His bones there whitening many a day,
Though sun and rain might work their will,
From bird and wolf protected still—

For he had one companion, one
Watched o'er him in the desert lone.
That faithful dog beside sat aye
Baying the vulture from his prey.
Else moved not, slept not, stirred not, still
O'er lake and mountain, rock and rill,
Rung his short, plaintive, timid cry
Most melancholy. None passed by,
None heard his sorrowing call for aid,
Yet still beside the corpse he stayed
And watched it molder, and the clay,
When three long months had passed away,
It was discovered where it lay
And he beside it. Would that we could love
As he did.

CHARLES BAUDELAIRE
(1821–1867)
Translated by Duncan Wu

BAUDELAIRE MUCH PREFERRED cats to dogs as daily companions, but when he visited Belgium and saw how badly dogs were treated—some were hitched to carts and made to pull them, while others were fodder for "the man who gets rich at fairs by eating live dogs"—he felt more warmly toward them, and was inspired to write "The Good Dogs," last of the *poèmes en prose* in *Paris Spleen*. It is in part an impassioned response to a decree at the beginning of Napoleon III's Second Empire (1852–1870) that all strays in Paris be rounded up and exterminated. Baudelaire begins with an address to the British novelist Laurence Sterne (1713–1768), famous for a dialogue in *Tristram Shandy* between Uncle Toby and the donkey who was blocking his path. Instead of thrashing the daylights out of it (the usual response at that unenlightened time), Toby gives it a macaroon, partly for the pleasure of watching the donkey eat it. Baudelaire wrote "The Good Dogs" in Brussels (a city he hated), where he saw working dogs cruelly treated by their owners; the artist Joseph Stevens, to whom Baudelaire dedicates the poem, depicted some in his paintings. (Stevens had owned the "waistcoat of rich, faded colors, reminiscent of autumnal suns, the beauty of mature women, and sultry summers in Saint-Martin in the Hautes-Pyrénées," which he gifted unhesitatingly to Baudelaire.) "The Dog and the Perfume Bottle" is more representative of Baudelaire's usual attitude to dogs: given the choice, he much preferred the company of cats.

The Dog and the Perfume Bottle

"Hey! Nice doggie, lovely doggie, come and take a whiff of this exquisite scent from the best perfumier in town."

And the furry animal, tail a-wag (the equivalent of a laugh and a wink), waddles over and rubs his ever-inquiring snout against the uncorked vial—and then, recoiling suddenly in horror, barks at me in reproach.

"Ha! Miserable stupid creature, had I presented you with a hatful of excrement, your moist black nose would have flared in ecstasy and you might well have scoffed the lot. In that respect, you, tawdry companion in my sad existence, resemble the general public, who should never be offered delicate odors, which are bound to annoy them, but instead a carefully selected range of dog faeces."

The Good Dogs

To Joseph Stevens[1]

I'm quite unembarrassed about my love for the writings of Georges-Louis Leclerc, Comte de Buffon,[2] even in front of young

---

1. Joseph Edouard Stevens (1814–1892) was an animal painter in Belgium. Stevens gave his waistcoat, mentioned in the poem, to Baudelaire when Baudelaire expressed admiration for it.   2. *Georges-Louis Leclerc, Comte de Buffon*: Buffon (1708–1788) was a naturalist and mathematician, famous for the remark: "Le style, c'est l'homme" (The style is the man).

writers, but today I'm not calling to my aid the soul of that magnificent artist of nature's grandeur—no. I would rather turn to Laurence Sterne, to whom I say: "Incomparable comedian of sentiment! Descend to me from the heavens, or rise up to me from the Elysian Fields, to inspire a prose poem worthy of you about the good dogs, the poor dogs. Return astride the famous donkey who in the eye of posterity will always be your companion, and above all ensure he has his immortal macaroon, carried delicately between his lips!"

To hell with the academic muse, I've no time for that prudish old cow! I invoke the commonplace muse, muse of urban life and the throbbingly alive, to help me praise the good dogs, the poor dogs, the wretched dogs, the dogs cast out as diseased and flea-ridden—though not by the impoverished, with whom they live, nor by the poet, who regards them with fraternal solidarity.

Fie upon the foppish and conceited dogs, whether Great Dane, King Charles, pug, or lapdog, so vain they hurl themselves into the innocent visitor's privates, certain they're the source of pleasure— as boisterous as a brat, stupid as a whore, surly and insolent as a servant. Fie, above all, on those four-legged serpents, those quivering layabouts called greyhounds whose pointy snouts lack the ability to trace a friend's scent, and whose flat skulls lack the intelligence to enable them even to play dominoes!

Back to their luxurious gated residences with these tiresome, sick-making parasites!

Yes, back to their silk-lined, well-appointed dog-mansions! I sing the mud-covered dog, the poor dog, the stray dog, the wandering dog, the street-performing dog, the dog whose instinct (like that of the penniless, the gypsy and the minstrel) is spurred magnificently by necessity, true mother and guardian of intelligence!

I sing calamitous dogs—those who wander solitary in the winding ravines of immense cities, or those whose twinkling, soulful eyes say to the derelict, "Take me with you, and out of our sadness we will forge a kind of happiness!"

"Where do dogs go?" Nestor Roqueplan[3] once asked in an immortal article he has doubtless forgotten, and which only myself (and perhaps Sainte-Beuve[4]) can now recall.

Where do dogs *go*? ask the inattentive and unobservant. Well, they tend to their affairs: business meetings, romantic assignations. Through the mist, the snow, the mud, in the heat of the day, through the dripping rain, they go, they come, they trot, they duck under carriages, roused by fleas, passion, need or duty. Like us, they rise early in the morning, earn their keep, or gallop to their pleasures.

Some sleep in a suburban foxhole, and come every day, at the same time, to beg at the kitchen door of the Palais Royal; others come in packs from over fifteen miles away, to share the meal prepared by those sexagenarian virgins whose unloved hearts are now devoted to animals, because imbecilic men have no further interest in them. There are other dogs who, like runaway slaves, mad for love, leave home to visit the big city and frolic for an hour with a glamorous, good-looking bitch, a trifle *distrait* in her appearance perhaps, but proud and grateful for the attention.

3. *Nestor Roqueplan*: Nestor Roqueplan (1805–1870) was a journalist and theater director.   4. *Saint-Beuve*: Charles Augustin Saint-Beuve (1804–1869) was a literary critic and an acquaintance of Baudelaire.

Though they don't have watches, diaries, or notebooks, they are always on time.

Do you know Belgium, that mecca of sloth? And have you admired, as I have, all its energetic dogs harnessed to the carts of the butcher, the milkman and the baker, who, in their triumphant barking, articulate the proud joy they feel in competing with one another, and in demonstrating the laziness and indolence of the horses?

Here are two even more civilized creatures. Let me show you the room of an absent circus entertainer. A painted wooden bed, no curtains, lice-infested blankets trailing across the floor, two chairs with straw seats, a cast-iron stove, and one or two broken musical instruments. What lamentable furnishings! But behold, I pray you, these two intelligent characters dressed in sumptuous costumes, a little worn, coiffed like troubadours or soldiers, who watch, with the fixed stare of a sorcerer, the potion "without a name" simmering on the stove, in which stands a long spoon like one of those masts erected to announce completion of a building.

Surely it's right such impassioned performers hit the road only when their stomachs are full of a substantial, robust broth? And won't you allow some bodily comfort to those poor devils who spend their days confronting an indifferent public and an unjust master who hogs the limelight and consumes more soup than four acrobats put together?

I've often reflected, fondly and affectionately, on those four-legged philosophers—helpful, submissive and devoted—who in republican terms might be described as "slave labor," if the republic, obsessed as it is with the welfare of humans, had the inclination to preserve the honor of dogs!

And how many times have I wondered whether there is a special place (who knows?) where such courage, patience and toil is rewarded—a special paradise for good dogs, poor dogs, mud-bespattered dogs, and sad dogs—just as Swedenborg[5] argued there is one heaven for the Turks and another for the Dutch.

As payment for their songs, the shepherds of Virgil and Theocritus[6] received a nice smelly cheese, a perfectly crafted flute, or a goat heavy with milk. The poet who sang the poor dogs has been given a waistcoat of rich, faded colors, reminiscent of autumnal suns, the voluptuous beauty of mature women, and sultry summers in Saint-Martin in the Hautes-Pyrénées. None of those present in the tavern of Rue Villa-Hermosa will forget the exuberance with which the painter removed his waistcoat in favor of the poet, knowing how right and just it was to champion the poor dogs. Just as a magnificent Italian tyrant once offered the divine Pietro Aretino either a dagger encrusted with precious gems or a court mantle in exchange for a priceless sonnet or an intriguing satirical poem.

When the poet puts on the painter's waistcoat, he has no choice but to think of the good dogs, philosophical dogs, the summers of St-Martin, and the gorgeousness of very mature women.

5. Emanuel Swedenborg (1688–1772) was a philosopher and mystic. 6. Virgil (70 BC–19 BC) and Theocritus (300 BC) were poets who wrote about rural life.

MATTHEW ARNOLD
(1822–1888)

A CRITIC, POET, and school inspector, Arnold is in many respects exemplary of the Victorian intellectual, but is given emotional depth by his love of animals. He famously elegized his pet canary in a poem that begins "Poor Matthias! Found him lying / Fallen beneath his perch and dying!"—a memorable opening couplet. Geist and Kaiser were dachshunds, apparently his favorite breed of dog, both of whom he memorialized in verse. Geist means "spirit" in German. The black dachshund was owned originally by Arnold's son, who, when he went to Australia, passed Geist on to his father. In London, Arnold would walk around Hyde Park with Geist; in the country, Geist would be let out so he could bark at the thrushes. Arnold owned two other dachshunds called Max and Kaiser. Though originally acquired as a dachshund, Kaiser clearly had some collie ancestry, which became more obvious as he got older.

Geist's Grave

Four years!—and didst thou stay above
The ground, which hides thee now, but four?

And all that life, and all that love,
Were crowded, Geist, into no more?

Only four years those winning ways,
Which make me for thy presence yearn,
Called us to pet thee or to praise,
Dear little friend! at every turn?

That loving heart, that patient soul,
Had they indeed no longer span,
To run their course, and reach their goal,
And read their homily to man?

That liquid, melancholy eye,
From whose pathetic, soul-fed springs
Seemed urging the Virgilian cry, [1]
The sense of tears in mortal things—

That steadfast, mournful strain, consoled
By spirits gloriously gay,
And temper of heroic mold—
What, was four years their whole short day?

Yes, only four!—and not the course
Of all the centuries yet to come,
And not the infinite resource
Of nature, with her countless sum

1. *The Virgilian cry*: "sunt lacrimae rerum et mentem mortalia tangunt" (Virgil, *Aeneid* 1.462).

Of figures, with her fullness vast
Of new creation evermore,
Can ever quite repeat the past,
Or just thy little self restore.

Stern law of every mortal lot!
Which man, proud man, finds hard to bear,
And builds himself I know not what
Of second life I know not where.

But thou, when struck thine hour to go,
On us, who stood despondent by,
A meek last glance of love didst throw,
And humbly lay thee down to die.

Yet would we keep thee in our heart—
Would fix our favorite on the scene,
Nor let thee utterly depart
And be as if thou ne'er hadst been.

And so there rise these lines of verse
On lips that rarely form them now;
While to each other we rehearse:
Such ways, such arts, such looks hadst thou!

We stroke thy broad brown paws again,
We bid thee to thy vacant chair,
We greet thee by the window-pane,
We hear thy scuffle on the stair.

We see the flaps of thy large ears
Quick raised to ask which way we go;
Crossing the frozen lake, appears
Thy small black figure on the snow!

Nor to us only art thou dear
Who mourn thee in thine English home;
Thou hast thine absent master's tear,
Dropped by the far Australian foam.

Thy memory lasts both here and there,
And thou shalt live as long as we.
And after that—thou dost not care!
In us was all the world to thee.

Yet, fondly zealous for thy fame,
Even to a date beyond our own
We strive to carry down thy name,
By mounded turf, and graven stone.

We lay thee, close within our reach,
Here, where the grass is smooth and warm,
Between the holly and the beech,
Where oft we watched thy couchant form,

Asleep, yet lending half an ear
To travelers on the Portsmouth road;—   2

2. *The Portsmouth road*: Arnold lived at Pains Hill in Cobham, which is on the road
that runs from London through Guildford and then to Portsmouth in Hampshire.

There build we thee, oh guardian dear,
Marked with a stone, thy last abode!

Then some, who through this garden pass,
When we too, like thyself, are clay,
Shall see thy grave upon the grass,
And stop before the stone, and say:

People who lived here long ago
Did by this stone, it seems, intend
To name for future times to know
The dachshund, Geist, their little friend.

Kaiser Dead

April 6, 1887

What, Kaiser dead? The heavy news
Post-haste to Cobham calls the muse,
From where in Farringford she brews
    The ode sublime,
Or with Pen-bryn's bold bard pursues[3]
    A rival rhyme.
Kai's bracelet tail, Kai's busy feet
Were known to all the village-street.
"What, poor Kai dead?" say all I meet;
    "A loss indeed!"
Oh for the croon pathetic, sweet
    Of Robin's reed!

3. **Pen-bryn's bold bard** Sir Lewis Morris (1833–1907)

Six years ago I brought him down,
A baby dog, from London town;
Round his small throat of black and brown
    A ribbon blue,
And vouched by glorious renown—
    A dachshund true.
His mother, most majestic dame,
Of blood unmixed from Potsdam came,
And Kaiser's race we deemed the same,
    No lineage higher.
And so he bore the imperial name;
    But ah, his sire!
Soon, soon the days conviction bring.
The collie hair, the collie swing,
The tail's indomitable ring,
    The eye's unrest—
The case was clear: a mongrel thing
    Kai stood confessed.
But all those virtues which commend
The humbler sort who serve and tend,
Were thine in store, thou faithful friend.
    What sense, what cheer!
To us, declining towards our end,
    A mate how dear!
For Max, thy brother dog, began
To flag, and feel his narrowing span.
And cold, besides, his blue blood ran,
    Since, 'gainst the classes,

He heard, of late, the Grand Old Man
    Incite the masses. ⁴

Yes, Max and we grew slow and sad;
But Kai, a tireless shepherd-lad,
Teeming with plans, alert, and glad
    In work or play,
Like sunshine went and came, and bade
    Live out the day!

Still, still I see the figure smart—
Trophy in mouth, agog to start,
Then home returned, once more depart;
    Or pressed together
Against thy mistress, loving heart,
    In winter weather.

I see the tail, like bracelet twirled,
In moments of disgrace uncurled,
Then at a pardoning word refurled,
    A conquering sign;
Crying, "Come on, and range the world,
    And never pine."

Thine eye was bright, thy coat it shone;
Thou hast thine errands, off and on;
In joy thy last morn flew; anon,
    A fit! All's over;

4. The Grand Old Man was William Ewart Gladstone (1809–1898), prime minister of Britain for four terms from 1868 to 1894. The Franchise Bill of 1884 extended the vote to all heads of households, including many agricultural laborers.

And thou art gone where Geist hath gone,
    And Toss, and Rover.
Poor Max, with downcast, reverent head,
Regards his brother's form outspread;
Full well Max knows the friend is dead
    Whose cordial talk
And jokes in doggish language said,
    Beguiled his walk.
And Glory, stretched at Burwood gate,
Thy passing by doth vainly wait;
And jealous Jock, thy only hate,
    The chiel from Skye,   5
Lets from his shaggy Highland pate
    Thy memory die.
Well fetch his graven collar fine,
And rub the steel, and make it shine,
And leave it round thy neck to twine,
    Kai, in thy grave.
There of thy master keep that sign,
    And this plain stave.

5. *chiel* young fellow

CHRISTINA ROSSETTI
(1830–1894)

IN ROSSETTI'S CASE, the term "animal-lover" would be an understatement. She kept a sizeable menagerie in her home, including a wombat. "He is a round furry ball with a head something between a bear and a guineapig, no legs, human feet with heels like anybody else and no tail," explained her brother Dante Gabriel Rossetti, "he follows one about like a dog." Christina was also a passionate anti-vivisectionist, and wrote a number of poems designed to illustrate the motto, "Hurt no living thing." She believed that, after death, we would be "confronted by any good or any evil we may have brought to such as these [animals]: not only by whatever we have done or left undone to the least of Christ's brethren, but even also to the least of His creatures." Though not exclusively about dogs, the poem below begins with a canine, and was written to help the anti-vivisectionist cause. She donated autograph manuscripts of it to an auction designed to raise money for anti-vivisectionists; all copies were sold.

A Poor Old Dog

Pity the sorrows of a poor old dog
    Who wags his tail a-begging in his need;
Despise not even the sorrows of a frog,
    God's creature too, and that's enough to plead;
Spare puss who trusts us dozing on our hearth;
    Spare bunny, once so frisky and so free;
Spare all the harmless creatures of the earth:
    Spare, and be spared—or who shall plead for thee?

EMILY DICKINSON
(1830–1886)

"YOU ASK OF my Companions," Dickinson wrote to her friend Thomas Wentworth Higginson in April 1862, "Hills—sir—and the Sundown, and a Dog large as myself, that my Father bought me." That was Carlo, a brown Newfoundland she was given in the winter of 1849–1850, whom she called her "Shaggy Ally." Her father hoped Carlo would help her overcome a dislike of going out in public: he accompanied her wherever she went and served as her confidante, with whom she discussed the things troubling her; "I think Carlo would please you," she told Higginson, "He is dumb and brave." Friends recalled her turning up at their door with the huge, bearlike, dark-furred creature slobbering in front of her. She was devoted to him, and through the worst of the American Civil War, received from him much psychological and emotional support. His death in January 1866 led her to become more reclusive. Writing to Higginson in June of that year, she thanked him for his kind words about the dog, and added: "Thank you, I wish for Carlo." She then copied out the second stanza of "They say that 'time assuages.'" The poem had been written in 1864, well before, so cannot have been inspired by Carlo's death, but the fact that she applies it to him leads me to think it should be included here. Dickinson never adopted another canine friend.

They say that "time assuages"

They say that "time assuages,"—
   Time never did assuage;
An actual suffering strengthens,
   As sinews do, with age.

Time is a test of trouble,
   But not a remedy.
If such it prove, it prove too
   There was no malady.

By the Sea

I started early, took my dog,
And visited the sea;
The mermaids in the basement
Came out to look at me,

And frigates in the upper floor
Extended hempen hands,
Presuming me to be a mouse
Aground, upon the sands.

But no man moved me till the tide
Went past my simple shoe,
And past my apron and my belt,
And past my bodice too,

And made as he would eat me up
As wholly as a dew
Upon a dandelion's sleeve—
And then I started too.

And he—he followed close behind;
I felt his silver heel
Upon my ankle,—then my shoes
Would overflow with pearl.

Until we met the solid town,
No man he seemed to know;
And bowing with a mighty look
At me, the sea withdrew.

THOMAS HARDY
(1840–1928)

THE MOST MEMORABLE of Hardy's many dogs was the dictatorial fox terrier Wessex, who treated Hardy's house, Max Gate in Dorchester, as his personal property. Visitors were greeted by him nipping—and often ripping—their clothing. At dinner, Wessex roamed the table—that's to say, *on* the table, helping himself to guests' food. Attempts to deter him were greeted with snarls, growls, and more nips. Hardy made no attempt to discourage him; indeed, he was greatly amused by Wessex's proprietorial attitude to other peoples' food. When he died, Hardy dug his grave and buried him, carving the headstone with his own hands.

Hardy believed passionately that animals should be kindly treated, and forbade his gardener from using any means to trap or shoot animals and birds, regardless of their consumption of fruit and vegetables. He wrote a letter to the *Times* deploring cruelty to animals, with this anecdote:

> I have been present at dog performances at country fairs, where the wretched animals so trembled with terror when they failed to execute the feat required of them that they could hardly stand, and remained with eyes of misery fixed upon their

master, paralysed at the knowledge of what was in store for them behind the scenes, whence their shrieks could afterwards be heard through the canvas.[1]

Hardy objected to keeping birds in cages and rabbits in hutches; denounced the use of drugs on animals and objected to blood sports.

"Ah, Are You Digging on My Grave?"

"Ah, are you digging on my grave,
    My loved one? Planting rue?"
"No. Yesterday he went to wed
One of the brightest wealth has bred.
'It cannot hurt her now,' he said,
    'That I should not be true.'"

"Then who is digging on my grave?
    My nearest dearest kin?"
"Ah, no: they sit and think, 'What use!
What good will planting flowers produce?
No tendance of her mound can loose
    Her spirit from Death's gin.'"

"But someone digs upon my grave?
    My enemy?—prodding sly?"
"Nay: when she heard you had passed the Gate

---

1. Harold Orel, *The Final Years of Thomas Hardy, 1912–1928* (London: Macmillan, 1976), p. 89.

That shuts on all flesh soon or late,
She thought you no more worth her hate,
  And cares not where you lie."

"Then, who is digging on my grave?
  Say—since I have not guessed!"
"Oh it is I, my mistress dear,
Your little dog, who still lives near,
And much I hope my movements here
  Have not disturbed your rest?"

"Ah, yes! You dig upon my grave . . .
  Why flashed it not on me
That one true heart was left behind!
What feeling do we ever find
To equal among humankind
  A dog's fidelity!"

"Mistress, I dug upon your grave
  To bury a bone, in case
I should be hungry near this spot
When passing on my daily trot.
I am sorry, but I quite forgot
  It was your resting-place."

AMBROSE BIERCE
(1842–ca. 1914)

"THE DOG IS a detestable quadruped," wrote Bierce, "He knows more ways to be unmentionable than can be suppressed in seven languages." Only seven? In case his meaning is unclear, his "Dissertation on Dogs" continues: "The dog is an encampment of fleas, and a reservoir of sinful smells." Bierce goes on to condemn not just dogs but the entire human race. Women, he tells us, "adore not only dogs, but Dog—not only their own horrible little beasts, but those of others. But women will love anything; they love men who love dogs." Not a fan, then, but Bierce was a great American poet—among the first—and "The Oakland Dog," one of his most memorable poems, is unlike any other in this anthology. Those of a nervous disposition may wish to turn away, but the rest of us, dog lovers or not, will find ourselves transfixed by his apocalyptic vision. "To a Stray Dog" shows a different side to Bierce—a sympathy expressed through the desire to rename a dog, from Towser to Goucher.

The Oakland Dog
I lay one happy night in bed
And dreamed that all the dogs were dead.

They'd all been taken out and shot—
Their bodies strewed each vacant lot.

O'er all the earth, from Berkeley down
To San Leandro's ancient town,
And out in space as far as Niles—
I saw their mortal parts in piles.

One stack upreared its ridge so high
Against the azure of the sky
That some good soul, with pious views,
Put up a steeple and sold pews.

No wagging tail the scene relieved:
I never in my life conceived
(I swear it on the Decalogue!)
Such penury of living dog.

The barking and the howling stilled,
The snarling with the snarler killed,
All nature seemed to hold its breath:
The silence was as deep as death.

True, candidates were all in roar
On every platform, as before;
And villains, as before, felt free
To finger the calliope.

True, the Salvationist by night,
And milkman in the early light,
The lonely flutist and the mill
Performed their functions with a will.

True, church bells on a Sunday rang
The sick man's curtain down—the bang
Of trains, contesting for the track,
Out of the shadow called him back.

True, cocks, at all unheavenly hours,
Crew with excruciating powers,
Cats on the woodshed rang and roared,
Fat citizens and foghorns snored.

But this was all too fine for ears
Accustomed, through the awful years,
To the nocturnal monologues
And day debates of Oakland dogs.

And so the world was silent. Now
What else befell—to whom and how?
Imprimis, then, there were no fleas,
And days of worth brought nights of ease.

Men walked about without the dread
Of being torn to many a shred,
Each fragment holding half a cruse
Of hydrophobia's quickening juice.

They had not to propitiate
Some curst kioodle at each gate,
But entered one another's grounds
Unscared, and were not fed to hounds.

Women could drive and not a pup
Would lift the horse's tendons up
And let them go—to interject
A certain musical effect.

Even children's ponies went about,
All grave and sober-paced, without
A bulldog hanging to each nose—
Proud of his fragrance, I suppose.

Dog being dead, Man's lawless flame
Burned out: he granted Woman's claim,
Children's and those of country, art—
They all took lodgings in his heart.

When memories of his former shame
Crimsoned his cheeks with sudden flame
He said, "I know my fault too well—
They fawned upon me and I fell."

Ah! 'twas a lovely world!—no more
I met that indisposing bore,
The unseraphic cynogogue—
The man who's proud to love a dog.

Thus in my dream the golden reign
Of Reason filled the world again,
And all mankind confessed her sway,
From Walnut Creek to San Jose.

To a Stray Dog

Well, Towser (I'm thinking your name must be Towser),
    You're a decentish puppy as puppydogs go,
For you never, I'm sure, could have dined upon trowser,
    And your tail's unimpeachably curled just so.

But, dear me! your name—if 'tis yours—is a "poser":
    Its meaning I cannot get anywise at,
When spoken correctly perhaps it is Toser,
    And means one who toses. Max Muller, how's that?

I ne'er was ingenious at all at divining
    A word's prehistorical, primitive state,
Or finding its root, like a mole, by consigning
    Its bloom to the turnep-top's sorrowful fate.

And, now that I think of it well, I'm no nearer
    The riddle's solution than ever—for how's
My pretty invented word, "tose," any clearer
    In point of its signification than "towse"?

So Towser (or Toser), I mean to rename you
    In honor of some good and eminent man,

In the light and the heat of whose quickening fame you
　　May grow to an eminent dog if you can.

In sunshine like his you'll not long be a croucher:
　　The Senate shall hear you—for that I will vouch.
Come here, sir. Stand up. I rechristen you Goucher.
　　But damn you! I'll shoot you if ever you gouch!

ANDREW "BANJO" PATERSON
(1864–1941)

ANDREW PATERSON—AN AUSTRALIAN of Scottish extraction—was the author of much-loved lyric poems of the Australian outback, most famously "Waltzing Matilda" (about a farm laborer who steals a sheep and commits suicide to avoid punishment for theft). Paterson began his professional life as a solicitor but early on began publishing poems in Sydney newspapers. His success as a poet led him to leave the legal profession and become a journalist. During the First World War, he served in France and Egypt. He also wrote stories, including "The Dog," which begins:

> The dog is a member of society who likes to have his day's work, and who does it more conscientiously than most human beings. A dog always looks as if he ought to have a pipe in his mouth and a black bag for his lunch, and then he would go quite happily to office every day.

High Explosive

'Twas the dingo pup to his dam that said,
"It's time I worked for my daily bread.

Out in the world I intend to go,
And you'd be surprised at the things I know.

There's a wild duck's nest in a sheltered spot,
And I'll go right down and I'll eat the lot."
But when he got to his destined prey
He found that the ducks had flown away.

But an egg was left that would quench his thirst,
So he bit the egg and it straightway burst.
It burst with a bang, and he turned and fled,
For he thought that the egg had shot him dead.

"Oh, mother," he said, "let us clear right out
Or we'll lose our lives with the bombs about;
And it's lucky I am that I'm not blown up—
It's a very hard life," said the dingo pup.

A Dog's Mistake

(In Doggerel Verse)

He had drifted in among us as a straw drifts with the tide,
He was just a wandering mongrel from the weary world outside;
He was not aristocratic, being mostly ribs and hair,
With a hint of spaniel parents and a touch of native bear.

He was very poor and humble and content with what he got,
So we fed him bones and biscuits, till he heartened up a lot;

Then he growled and grew aggressive, treating orders with
    disdain,
Till at last he bit the butcher, which would argue want of brain.

Now the butcher, noble fellow, was a sport beyond belief,
And instead of bringing actions he brought half a shin of beef,
Which he handed on to Fido, who received it as a right
And removed it to the garden, where he buried it at night.

'Twas the means of his undoing, for my wife, who'd stood his
    friend,
To adopt a slang expression, "went in off the deepest end,"
For among the pinks and pansies, the gloxinias and the gorse
He had made an excavation like a graveyard for a horse.

Then we held a consultation which decided on his fate:
'Twas in anger more than sorrow that we led him to the gate,
And we handed him the beef-bone as provision for the day,
Then we opened wide the portal and we told him, "On your way."

RUDYARD KIPLING
(1865–1936)

"THE POWER OF the Dog" may be the best-known poem in this volume; it could only have been written by someone who had observed dogs closely and with love. Kipling's favorite breed was the Aberdeen terrier (often called "Scotties"), which he cast as Boots, narrator of *Thy Servant a Dog*. It sold one hundred thousand copies in 1930. The death of an actual dog, Wop the Scottie, inspired "Four-Feet," included below. Kipling's correspondence of the late 1920s is full of stories about Wop; in December 1929 he described Wop's splendid new red collar with matching lead, and in May 1930, recounted how the misapprehension that he was about to leave Bateman's (his home) led the dog to cry: "I didn't know dogs wept. I know I nearly did."

Four-Feet

I have done mostly what most men do,
And pushed it out of my mind;
But I can't forget, if I wanted to,
Four-Feet trotting behind.

Day after day, the whole day through—
Wherever my road inclined—
Four-Feet said, "I am coming with you!"
And trotted along behind.

Now I must go by some other round,—
Which I shall never find—
Somewhere that does not carry the sound
Of Four-Feet trotting behind.

The Power of the Dog

There is sorrow enough in the natural way
From men and women to fill our day;
And when we are certain of sorrow in store,
Why do we always arrange for more?
Brothers and sisters, I bid you beware
Of giving your heart to a dog to tear.

Buy a pup and your money will buy
Love unflinching that cannot lie—
Perfect passion and worship fed
By a kick in the ribs or a pat on the head.
Nevertheless it is hardly fair
To risk your heart for a dog to tear.

When the fourteen years which nature permits
Are closing in asthma, or tumour, or fits,
And the vet's unspoken prescription runs
To lethal chambers or loaded guns,

Then you will find—it's your own affair—
But . . . you've given your heart for a dog to tear.

When the body that lived at your single will,
With its whimper of welcome, is stilled (how still!);
When the spirit that answered your every mood
Is gone—wherever it goes—for good,
You will discover how much you care,
And will give your heart to a dog to tear.

We've sorrow enough in the natural way,
When it comes to burying Christian clay.
Our loves are not given, but only lent,
At compound interest of cent per cent.
Though it is not always the case, I believe,
That the longer we've kept 'em, the more do we grieve:

For when debts are payable, right or wrong,
A short-time loan is as bad as a long—
So why in Heaven (before we are there)
Should we give our hearts to a dog to tear?

ROBERT FROST
(1874–1963)

FROST OWNED DOGS throughout his life, the last was Gillie, a black-and-white border collie of Scottish descent who was his sole companion after his wife, Elinor, died of cancer. Frost acquired Gillie in 1939, who was from the start a companion on Frost's walks through the Vermont countryside. In May of that year, Frost took up the Ralph Waldo Emerson Fellowship in Poetry at Harvard, and he and Gillie became frequently glimpsed figures in the streets of Cambridge.

Canis Major

The great Overdog
That heavenly beast
With a star in one eye
Gives a leap in the east.
He dances upright
All the way to the west
And never once drops
On his forefeet to rest.
I'm a poor underdog,

But tonight I will bark
With the great Overdog
That romps through the dark.

The Span of Life

The old dog barks backward without getting up.
I can remember when he was a pup.

EDWARD THOMAS
(1878–1917)

THOMAS GREW UP with dogs and was particularly attached to Rags, the Irish terrier he and his wife owned. In 1904, he would take long walks with Rags and author Arthur Ransome around Bearsted Green, in Kent, where he then lived. Rags must often have accompanied Thomas around the village of Dymock in Gloucestershire. In November 1914, he encountered a "short stiffish oldish man" with a "small brown bitch," who followed his master everywhere. Among other things, the man told Thomas he was "thinking about soldiers in France—terrible affair in cold weather." That encounter was the basis of "Man and Dog."

Man and Dog

"'Twill take some getting." "Sir, I think 'twill so."
The old man stared up at the mistletoe
That hung too high in the poplar's crest for plunder
Of any climber, though not for kissing under:
Then he went on against the north-east wind—
Straight but lame, leaning on a staff new-skinned,
Carrying a brolly, flag-basket, and old coat—
Towards Alton, ten miles off. And he had not

Done less from Chilgrove where he pulled up docks.
'Twere best, if he had had "a money-box,"
To have waited there till the sheep cleared a field
For what a half-week's flint-picking would yield.
His mind was running on the work he had done
Since he left Christchurch in the New Forest, one
Spring in the seventies—navvying on dock and line
From Southampton to Newcastle-on-Tyne—
In seventy-four a year of soldiering
With the Berkshires—hoeing and harvesting
In half the shires where corn and couch will grow.
His sons, three sons, were fighting, but the hoe
And reap-hook he liked, or anything to do with trees.
He fell once from a poplar tall as these:
The Flying Man they called him in hospital.
"If I flew now, to another world I'd fall."
He laughed and whistled to the small brown bitch
With spots of blue that hunted in the ditch.
Her foxy Welsh grandfather must have paired
Beneath him. He kept sheep in Wales and scared
Strangers, I will warrant, with his pearl eye
And trick of shrinking off as he were shy,
Then following close in silence for—for what?
"No rabbit, never fear, she ever got,
Yet always hunts. Today she nearly had one:
She would and she wouldn't. 'Twas like that. The bad one!
She's not much use, but still she's company,
Though I'm not. She goes everywhere with me.
So Alton I must reach tonight somehow:

I'll get no shakedown with that bedfellow
From farmers. Many a man sleeps worse tonight
Than I shall." "In the trenches." "Yes, that's right.
But they'll be out of that—I hope they be—
This weather, marching after the enemy."
"And so I hope. Good luck." And there I nodded
"Goodnight. You keep straight on." Stiffly he plodded;
And at his heels the crisp leaves scurried fast,
And the leaf-coloured robin watched. They passed,
The robin till next day, the man for good,
Together in the twilight of the wood.

Two Houses

Between a sunny bank and the sun
The farmhouse smiles
On the riverside plat:
No other one
So pleasant to look at
And remember, for many miles,
So velvet-hushed and cool under the warm tiles.

Nor far from the road it lies, yet caught
Far out of reach
Of the road's dust
And the dusty thought
Of passers-by, though each
Stops, and turns, and must
Look down at it like a wasp at the muslined peach.

But another house stood there long before:
And as if above graves
Still the turf heaves
Above its stones:
Dark hangs the sycamore,
Shadowing kennel and bones
And the black dog that shakes his chain and moans.

And when he barks, over the river
Flashing fast,
Dark echoes reply,
And the hollow past
Half yields the dead that never
More than half hidden lie:
And out they creep and back again for ever.

WILLIAM CARLOS WILLIAMS
(1883–1963)

If I were a dog
I'd sit down on a cold pavement
in the rain
if it so pleased me ... ("'To my Friend Ezra Pound," 1956)

IT'S HARD TO think of lines that so perfectly demonstrate an empathy with dogs. But then, empathy was Williams's strong suit—he was brought up in the school of John Keats (an influence he would later deny), who boasted of being able to enter even the world of a billiard ball, feeling "a sense of delight from its own roundness, smoothness, volubility, and the rapidity of its motion." Scholar Barry Ahearn observes that "'Smell!' is based on the everyday chore of urban or suburban householders—having to walk their dog: "Everywhere in the poem where the word 'nose' appears we could readily substitute 'dog.' The poem records the affectionate but impatient and sometimes exasperated remarks of a dog owner—with the regular replacement of 'dog' by 'nose.'"

Smell!

Oh strong-ridged and deeply hollowed
nose of mine! what will you not be smelling?
What tactless asses we are, you and I, boney nose,
always indiscriminate, always unashamed,
and now it is the souring flowers of the bedraggled
poplars: a festering pulp on the wet earth
beneath them. With what deep thirst
we quicken our desires
to that rank odor of a passing springtime!
Can you not be decent? Can you not reserve your ardors
for something less unlovely? What girl will care
for us, do you think, if we continue in these ways?
Must you taste everything? Must you know everything?
Must you have a part in everything?

EZRA POUND

(1885–1972)

BOTH POEMS HERE date from 1914; they are epigrammatic and have in common an ambiguity of tone—indeed, they are both, to a certain extent, comic. "The Seeing Eye" is really about the ability to observe closely—as Pound himself put it, "When I say they hadn't the 'seein' eye', I mean that they never succeeded in conveying the visual appearance of any one of their characters as distinct from any other. There was an almost complete lack of detail" ("Indiscretions"). In the last stanza of the poem, he refers to Chinese philosopher Tsin-Tsu, who never actually existed. The second poem included here, "Meditatio," appeared in an anthology of children's literature as recently as 1984, but it is not recommended for young readers. It has also been presented as the work of a Chinese poet, but it is definitely not that either. What is it, then? Obscene? Pound's publisher, Elkin Mathews, thought so; he deleted both "The Seeing Eye" and "Meditatio" from Pound's *Lustra* (1916) because he thought them "very nasty." In the end he published eight hundred copies without them and a shorter run of two hundred containing them, for private circulation only.

The Seeing Eye

The small dogs look at the big dogs;
They observe unwieldly dimensions
And curious imperfections of odor.

Here is a formal male group:
The young men look upon their seniors,
They consider the elderly mind
And observe its inexplicable correlations.

Said Tsin-Tsu:
It is only in small dogs and the young
That we find minute observation.

Meditatio

When I carefully consider the curious habits of dogs,
I am compelled to admit
That man is the superior animal.

When I consider the curious habits of man,
I confess, my friend, I am puzzled.

FRANCES CORNFORD
(1886–1960)

CORNFORD WAS BORN into the intellectually vibrant world of Cambridge University in England. She was one of a group of intellectuals that included Bertrand Russell, Eric Gill, and Rupert Brooke. *Poems* (1910), her first poetry collection, contains her most famous poem, "To a Fat Lady Seen from a Train"; *Spring Morning* followed in 1915, and *Autumn Midnight* in 1923. Often considered a children's writer, her poems nonetheless have a tendency to be sharp-edged and uncompromising—which explains their freshness today.

A Child's Dream

I had a little dog, and my dog was very small;
He licked me in the face, and he answered to my call;
Of all the treasures that were mine, I loved him most of all.

His nose was fresh as morning dew and blacker than the night;
I thought that it could even snuff the shadows and the light;
And his tail he held bravely, like a banner in a fight.

His body covered thick with hair was very good to smell;
His little stomach underneath was pink as any shell;
And I loved him and honoured him, more than words can tell.

We ran out in the morning, both of us, to play,
Up and down across the fields for all the sunny day;
But he ran so swiftly—he ran right away.

I looked for him, I called for him, entreatingly. Alas,
The dandelions could not speak, though they had seen him pass,
And nowhere was his waving tail among the waving grass.

I called him in a thousand ways and yet he did not come;
The pathways and the hedges were horrible and dumb.
I prayed to God who never heard. My desperate soul grew numb.

The sun sank low. I ran; I prayed: "If God has not the power
To find him, let me die. I cannot bear another hour."
When suddenly I came upon a great yellow flower.

And all among its petals, such was Heaven's grace,
In that golden hour, in that golden place,
All among its petals, was his hairy face.

Night Song
On moony nights the dogs bark shrill
Down the valley and up the hill.

There's one is angry to behold
The moon so unafraid and cold,
Who makes the earth as bright as day,
But yet unhappy, dead, and grey.

Another in his strawy lair
Says: "Who's a-howling over there?
By heavens I will stop him soon
From interfering with the moon."

So back he barks, with throat upthrown:
"You leave our moon, our moon alone."
And other distant dogs respond
Beyond the fields, beyond, beyond.

SIEGFRIED SASSOON
(1886–1967)

Sassoon had just turned away the one person he would ever truly love, Stephen Tennant, and announced his engagement to Hester Gatty, when his friend Rosamond Lehmann decided to give him Sheltie, the Dandie Dinmont terrier he had long adored. It was 1933. Years later, in June 1942, he was heartbroken at being told it would be most humane, given the dog's state of health, to have him put to sleep. Sheltie was, as he says in "Man and Dog," "One decent thing" in his life.

Man and Dog

Who's this—alone with stone and sky?
It's only my old dog and I—
It's only him; it's only me;
Alone with stone and grass and tree.

What share we most—we two together?
Smells, and awareness of the weather.
What is it makes us more than dust?
My trust in him; in me his trust.

Here's anyhow one decent thing
That life to man and dog can bring;
One decent thing, remultiplied
Till earth's last dog and man have died.

T. S. ELIOT
(1888–1965)

"OF COURSE, THE Yorkshire Terriers are only a makeshift," Eliot told a correspondent in 1932, the year he wrote "Lines" below, "when I retire to the country I intend to breed Blue Bedlingtons" (letter of October 20, 1932). For him, the Bedlington terrier was a near-obsession; he commanded the publisher, poet, and radical, Nancy Cunard, to breed them (letter of June 21, 1928). But as long as he was in London, Yorkies were his passion. In 1919 a small stray Yorkie followed Eliot through the rainswept streets of Bloomsbury; when he arrived home, he opened the door, and it shot into the three-room flat he shared with his wife Vivienne. They called it Dinah Brooks. In 1924 they acquired two more Yorkies named Peter and Polly Louise. "Lines to a Yorkshire Terrier" is the second of his *Five-Finger Exercises*.

Lines to a Yorkshire Terrier

In a brown field stood a tree
And the tree was crookt and dry.
In a black sky, from a green cloud
Natural forces shriek'd aloud,
Screamed, rattled, muttered endlessly.

Little dog was safe and warm
Under a cretonne eiderdown,
Yet the field was cracked and brown
And the tree was cramped and dry.
Pollicle dogs and cats all must
Jellicle cats and dogs all must
Like undertakers, come to dust.
Here a little dog I pause
Heaving up my prior paws,
Pause, and sleep endlessly.

GEOFFREY DEARMER
(1893–1996)

DEARMER FOUGHT IN Gallipoli for about four months during The First World War, and it must have been there he composed what remains the best known of his war poems, which describes an encounter with a formidable-looking dog while reconnoitering between the British and Turkish lines.

The Turkish Trench Dog

Night held me as I crawled and scrambled near
The Turkish lines. Above, the mocking stars
Silvered the curving parapet, and clear
Cloud-latticed beams o'erflecked the land with bars;
I, crouching, lay between
Tense-listening armies peering through the night,
Twin giants bound by tentacles unseen.
Here in dim-shadowed light
I saw him, as a sudden movement turned
His eyes towards me, glowing eyes that burned
A moment ere his snuffling muzzle found
My trail; and then as serpents mesmerize
He chained me with these unrelenting eyes,

That muscle-sliding rhythm, knit and bound
In spare-limbed symmetry, those perfect jaws,
And soft-approaching pitter-patter paws.
Nearer and nearer like a wolf he crept—
That moment had my swift revolver leapt—
But terror seized me, terror born of shame
Brought flooding revelation. For he came
As one who offers comradeship deserved,
An open ally of the human race,
And sniffing at my prostrate form unnerved
He licked my face!

DOROTHY PARKER
(1893–1967)

"I LOVE A big yard full of dogs," Parker once declared—and however many times her love affairs and marriages went wrong, she was seldom without one. She adored them, and they certainly adored her. At various times her household included a Boston terrier called Woodrow Wilson, a dachshund called Fraulein, and a poodle called Cliché, among many others. On one occasion, after one of her dogs threw up on someone's rug, having overindulged on foie gras, Parker turned to her hostess and remarked, "It's the company." On another, when her dog relieved herself copiously in the lobby of the Beverly Hills Hotel, the manager ran up to her pointing at the steaming, semi-liquid mess, shouting, "Miss Parker, Miss Parker! Look what your dog did!" Without hesitation, she turned to him, said "*I* did it," and walked smartly in the other direction. Bored and lonely in the south of France, she acquired a Scottie called Daisy, who responded to her name by looking contemptuously at whoever had just said it. Convinced this was a sign of intelligence, Parker exclaimed, "Why, that dog is practically a Phi Beta Kappa" (the oldest of the academic honor societies in the United States); "She can sit up and beg, and she can give her paw—I don't say she will, but she *can*." The poems below come from early in her career, the first from *Life* in 1921, the second from 1924.

My Dog

I often wonder why on earth
    You rate yourself so highly;
A shameless parasite, from birth
    You've lived the life of Reilly.
No claims to fame distinguish you;
    Your talents are not many;
You're constantly unfaithful to
    Your better self—if any.
Yet you believe, with faith profound,
    The world revolves about you;
May I point out, it staggered round
    For centuries without you?

In beauty, you're convinced you lead,
    While others only follow.
You think you look like Wallace Reid,
    Or, at the least, Apollo.
The fatal charms with which you're blest,
    You fancy, spell perfection;
The notion, may I not suggest,
    Is open to correction?
An alien streak your tail betrays;
    Your ears aren't what they would be;

Your mother was—forgive the phrase—
    No better than she should be.

One can but feel your gaiety
    Is somewhat over-hearty;
You take it on yourself to be
    The life of every party.
In bearing, while no doubt sincere,
    You're frankly, too informal.
And mentally, I sometimes fear,
    You're slightly under normal.
The least attention turns your brain,
    Repressions slip their tether;
Pray spare your friends the nervous strain
    And pull yourself together!

You take no thought for others' good
    In all your daily dealings,
I ask you, as a mother would,
    Where *are* your finer feelings?
I think I've seldom run across
    A life so far from lawful;
Your manners are a total loss,
    Your morals, something awful.
Perhaps you'll ask, as many do,
    What I endure your thrall for?
'Twas ever thus—it's such as you
    That women always fall for.

Verse for a Certain Dog

Such glorious faith as fills your limpid eyes,
>Dear little friend of mine, I never knew.
All-innocent are you, and yet all-wise.
>(For heaven's sake, stop worrying that shoe!)
You look about, and all you see is fair;
>This mighty globe was made for you alone.
Of all the thunderous ages, you're the heir.
>(Get off the pillow with that dirty bone!)

A skeptic world you face with steady gaze;
>High in young pride you hold your noble head;
Gayly you meet the rush of roaring days.
>(*Must* you eat puppy biscuit on the bed?)
Lancelike your courage, gleaming swift and strong,
>Yours the white rapture of a wingéd soul,
Yours is a spirit like a May-day song.
>(God help you, if you break the goldfish bowl!)

"Whatever is, is good," your gracious creed.
>You wear your joy of living like a crown.
Love lights your simplest act, your every deed.
>(Drop it, I tell you—put that kitten down!)
You are God's kindliest gift of all,—a friend;
>Your shining loyalty unflecked by doubt,
You ask but leave to follow to the end.
>(Now I suppose I've got to take you out!)

ROBERT GRAVES
(1895–1985)

GRAVES HAD JUST left Charterhouse School when the First World War broke out. He joined the Royal Welch Fusiliers and was sent to the Somme. On July 19, 1916, he was wounded by an exploding shell that tore through his body, nearly killing him. He was bandaged in the dressing-station and left for dead, and his commanding officer wrote immediately to his parents informing them of his demise. The *Times* reported his death on August 3. But he was far from dead and would recover and return to the front, only to be hospitalized with shell shock in 1917. *Over the Brazier*, his first collection of poems, was published in London in May 1916. "The First Funeral" evokes the trauma connected with his wartime experiences.

The First Funeral

(*The first corpse I saw was on the German
wires, and couldn't be buried.*)

The whole field was so smelly;
    We smelt the poor dog first:
His horrid swollen belly
    Looked just like going burst.

His fur was most untidy;
>He hadn't any eyes.
It happened on Good Friday
>And there was lots of flies.

And then I felt the coldest
>I'd ever felt, and sick,
But Rose, 'cause she's the oldest,
>Dared poke him with her stick.

He felt quite soft and horrid:
>The flies buzzed round his head
And settled on his forehead:
>Rose whispered: "That dog's dead.

You bury all dead people,
>When they're quite really dead,
Round churches with a steeple:
>Let's bury this," Rose said.

"And let's put mint all round it
>To hide the nasty smell."
I went to look and found it—
>Lots, growing near the well.

We poked him through the clover
>Into a hole, and then
We threw brown earth right over
>And said: "Poor dog, Amen!"

STEVIE SMITH
(1902–1971)

SMITH WAS RESPONSIBLE for a glossy book of cat photographs called *Cats in Color* (1960) in which she remarks: "I think all animal life, tamed or wild, the cat life, the dog life and the tiger life alike, are hidden from us and protected by darkness, they are too dark for us to read.... They are not ours to possess and know, they belong to another world and from that world and its strange obediences no human being can steal them away." This has to be one of the most eloquent accounts of the essential otherness not only of domestic animals but of wild animals, and the manner in which cats and dogs seem to enter our lives as visitors from another place. Smith's dog poems are as acutely sensitive to the eccentricity and inexplicable strangeness of canids. "O Pug!" is certainly a poem that is hard to forget; it is also one of the last written by Smith about the dog owned by her friends Anna and Michael Browne.

O Pug!

to the Brownes' pug dog, on my lap, in their
car, coming home from Norfolk

O Pug, some people do not like you,
But I like you,

Dog-eared

Some people say you do not breathe, you snore,
I don't mind,
One person says he is always conscious of your behind,
Is that your fault?

Your own people love you,
All the people in the family that owns you
Love you: Good pug, they cry, Happy pug,
Pug-come-for-a-walk.

You are an old dog now
And in all your life
You have never had cause for a moment's anxiety,
Yet,
In those great eyes of yours,
Those liquid and protuberant orbs,
Lies the shadow of immense insecurity. There
Panic walks.

Yes, yes, I know,
When your mistress is with you,
When your master
Takes you upon his lap,
Just then, for a moment,
Almost you are not frightened.

But at heart you are frightened, you always have been.

O Pug, obstinate old nervous breakdown,
In the midst of so much love,
And such comfort,
Still to feel unsafe and be afraid,

How one's heart goes out to you!

LOUIS MACNEICE
(1907–1963)

IN A LETTER from 1933, Macneice told Anthony Blunt, "Betsy is lame & I am having a painful time helping her round in the snow." This is just one reference among many to an assortment of dogs owned by Macneice and his wife, Mary. Betsy was a borzoi who liked to be lifted over stiles and was mocked by the local children as a "sissy dog." Macneice and Mary also had an Old English sheepdog called Cherry and a pug called Prunella. He recalled in his autobiography, "Each week we bought two weekly dog-papers and read the reports of the shows." In time they began to show their dogs at "Birmingham, Manchester, Cheltenham, Oxford, and Maidenhead, at Ranelagh, Cruft's and the Crystal Palace." Editors of Macneice's correspondence report a collection of "dog letters . . . which feature mock postcards and letters . . . between dogs, as well as many letters pertaining to the breeding and showing of dogs with the Kennel Club and Tail Waggers Club." Dogs feature in a number of Macneice's poems, including "The Individualist Speaks," "Wolves," "The Libertine," and "The Taxis."

Dogs in the Park

The precise yet furtive etiquette of dogs
Makes them ignore the whistle while they talk
In circles round each other, one-man bonds
Deferred in pauses of this man-made walk
To open vistas to a past of packs

That raven round the stuccoed terraces
And scavenge at the mouth of Stone Age caves;
What man proposes dog on his day disposes
In litter round both human and canine graves,
Then lifts his leg to wash the gravestones clean,

While simultaneously his eyes express
Apology and contempt; his master calls
And at the last and sidelong he returns,
Part heretic, part hack, and jumps and crawls
And fumbles to communicate and fails.

And then they leave the park, the leads are snapped
On to the spiky collars, the tails wag
For no known reason and the ears are pricked
To search through legendary copse and crag
For legendary creatures doomed to die
Even as they, the dogs, were doomed to live.

WILLIAM STAFFORD
(1914–1993)

"Do BIG DOGS have more importance than little dogs? And people?," Stafford asked himself on October 23, 1991.

How It Began

They struggled their legs and blindly loved, those puppies
inside my jacket as I walked through town. They crawled
for warmth and licked each other —their poor mother
dead, and one kind boy to save them. I spread
my arms over their world and hurried along.

At Ellen's place I knocked and waited—the tumult
invading my sleeves, all my jacket alive.
When she came to the door we tumbled—black, white,
gray, hungry—all over the living room floor
together, rolling, whining, happy and blind.

GWENDOLYN BROOKS
(1917–2000)

Vern

When walking in a tiny rain
Across the vacant lot,
A pup's a good companion—
If a pup you've got.

And when you've had a scold,
And no one loves you very,
And you cannot be merry,
A pup will let you look at him,
And even let you hold
His little wiggly warmness—

And let you snuggle down beside,
Nor mock the tears you have to hide.

LAWRENCE FERLINGHETTI
(b. 1919)

Dog

The dog trots freely in the street
and sees reality
and the things he sees
are bigger than himself
and the things he sees
are his reality
Drunks in doorways
Moons on trees
The dog trots freely thru the street
and the things he sees
are smaller than himself
Fish on newsprint
Ants in holes
Chickens in Chinatown windows
their heads a block away
The dog trots freely in the street
and the things he smells
smell something like himself

The dog trots freely in the street
past puddles and babies
cats and cigars
poolrooms and policemen
He doesn't hate cops
He merely has no use for them
and he goes past them
and past the dead cows hung up whole
in front of the San Francisco Meat Market
He would rather eat a tender cow
than a tough policeman
though either might do
And he goes past the Romeo Ravioli Factory
and past Coit's Tower   1
and past Congressman Doyle of the Unamerican Committee   2
He's afraid of Coit's Tower
but he's not afraid of Congressman Doyle
although what he hears is very discouraging
very depressing
very absurd
to a sad young dog like himself
to a serious dog like himself
His own fleas to eat
He will not be muzzled
Congressman Doyle is just another

1. Coit Tower stands over two hundred feet high in the Telegraph Hill
neighborhood of San Francisco.   2. Congressman Clyde Doyle (1887–1963), a
Democrat, served on the House Un-American Activities Committee from 1951
until his death.

fire hydrant
to him
The dog trots freely in the street
and has his own dog's life to live
and to think about
and to reflect upon
touching and tasting and testing everything
investigating everything
without benefit of perjury
a real realist
with a real tale to tell
and a real tail to tell it with
a real live
    barking
    democratic dog
engaged in real
    free enterprise
with something to say
    about ontology
something to say
    about reality
    and how to see it
    and how to hear it
with his head cocked sideways
    at streetcorners
as if he is just about to have
    his picture taken
    for Victor Records
    listening for

Dog-eared

His Master's Voice
and looking
like a living questionmark
into the
great gramophone
of puzzling existence
with its wondrous hollow horn
which always seems
just about to spout forth
some Victorious answer
to everything

HOWARD NEMEROV
(1920–1991)

IN HIS "DIGRESSION on Dogs," Nemerov writes entertainingly about Suzy, his beagle, and the "crew of wretched opportunists" who lived nearby—Klaus the dachshund, Ranger and Ginger (who "went from house to house at feeding time"), and Clancy who had only three legs ("the result of surgery which saved his life after he had been, doubtless through his own fault, hit by a car"). Nemerov's son, Alexander, tells me that "the dog about whom 'Walking the Dog' was written was Snifkin, a beagle-hound mix who got his Dostoevsky-like name from my dad himself. Snifkin was in St Louis; Suzy, from much earlier (before I was born), lived with the family in Bennington, Vermont."

Walking the Dog

Two universes mosey down the street
Connected by love and a leash and nothing else.
Mostly I look at lamplight through the leaves
While he mooches along with tail up and snout down,
Getting a secret knowledge through the nose
Almost entirely hidden from my sight.

Dog-eared

We stand while he's enraptured by a bush
Till I can't stand our standing any more
And haul him off; for our relationship
Is patience balancing to this side tug
And that side drag; a pair of symbionts
Contented not to think each other's thoughts.

What else we have in common's what he taught,
Our interest in shit. We know its every state
From steaming fresh through stink to nature's way
Of sluicing it downstreet dissolved in rain
Or drying it to dust that blows away.
We move along the street inspecting shit.

His sense of it is keener far than mine,
And only when he finds the place precise
He signifies by sniffing urgently
And circles thrice about, and squats, and shits,
Whereon we both with dignity walk home
And just to show who's master I write the poem.

VERNON SCANNELL
(1922–2007)

SCANNELL'S FAMILY SETTLED for a while in Ballaghaderreen, County Roscommon, in Ireland, in the mid-1920s, where, as a small boy, he took home the body of a dog he found in the streets. Scannell's friend and executor Martin Reed remembers: "Vernon often had a dog with him when I met him. I remember one called Robinson (named after the boxer of course) who dug a large hole in my garden though its owner denied all responsibility; and a delightful whippet called Hetta who kept him company for many years in Otley. She appears in a film I made about Vernon in 1991."

Dead Dog

One day I found a lost dog in the street.
The hairs about its grin were spiked with blood,
And it lay still as stone. It must have been
A little dog, for though I only stood
Nine inches for each one of my four years
I picked it up and took it home. My mother
Squealed, and later father spaded out
A bed and tucked my mongrel down in mud.

Dog-eared

I can't remember any feeling but
A moderate pity, cool not swollen-eyed;
Almost a godlike feeling now it seems.
My lump of dog was ordinary as bread.
I have no recollection of the school
Where I was taught my terror of the dead.

GALWAY KINNELL
(1927–2014)

Burning

He lives, who last night flopped from a log
Into the creek, and all night by an ankle
Lay pinned to the flood, dead as a nail
But for the skin of the teeth of his dog.

I brought him boiled eggs and broth.
He coughed and waved his spoon
And sat up saying he would dine alone,
Being fatigue itself after that bath.

I sat without in the sun with the dog.
Wearing a stocking on the ailing foot,
In monster crutches, he hobbled out,
And addressed the dog in bitter rage.

He told the yellow hound, his rescuer,
Its heart was bad, and it ought

Not wander by the creek at night;
If all his dogs got drowned he would be poor.

He stroked its head and disappeared in the shed
And came out with a stone mallet in his hands
And lifted that rocky weight of many pounds
And let it lapse on top of the dog's head.

I carted off the carcass, dug it deep.
Then he came too with what a thing to lug,
Or pour on a dog's grave, his thundermug,
And poured it out and went indoors to sleep.

FLEUR ADCOCK
(b. 1934)

A Surprise in the Peninsula

When I came in that night I found
the skin of a dog stretched flat and
nailed upon my wall between the
two windows. It seemed freshly killed—
there was blood at the edges. Not
my dog: I have never owned one,
I rather dislike them. (Perhaps
whoever did it knew that.) It
was a light brown dog, with smooth hair;
no head, but the tail still remained.
On the flat surface of the pelt
was branded the outline of the
peninsula, singed in thick black
strokes into the fur: a coarse map.
The position of the town was
marked by a bullet-hole; it went
right through the wall. I placed my eye
to it, and could see the dark trees

outside the house, flecked with moonlight.
I locked the door then, and sat up
all night, drinking small cups of the
bitter local coffee. A dog
would have been useful, I thought, for
protection. But perhaps the one
I had been given performed that
function; for no one came that night,
nor for three more. On the fourth day
it was time to leave. The dog-skin
still hung on the wall, stiff and dry
by now, the flies and the smell gone.
Could it, I wondered, have been meant
not as a warning, but a gift?
And, scarcely shuddering, I drew
the nails out and took it with me.

FREDERICK SEIDEL
(b. 1936)

The Little White Dog

The way the rain won't fall
Applies a velvet pressure, voice-off.
The held-back heaviness too sweet, the redolence,
Brings back the memory.

Life watches, watches,
From the control room, through the soundproof window,
With the sound turned off,
The orchestra warming up, playing scales.

It listens to the glistening.
The humidity reels, headier than methanol.
Treelined sidestreets, prick up your leaves.
The oboe is giving the *la* to the orchestra.

Someone shoots his cuffs to show his cufflinks,
Yellow gold to match his eyes, and pays the check.

Someone else is eight years old.
Her humility is volatile.

And when they kiss, he can't quite breathe.
The electric clouds perspire.
It's meteorology, it's her little dress, it's her violin,
It's unafraid. It's about to.

A sudden freshness stirs then stills the air, the century.
The new jet-black conductor raises her baton.
The melody of a little white dog,
Dead long ago, starts the soft spring rain.

CHARLES SIMIC
(b. 1938)

I GREW UP with stray dogs. It was during the Second World War in a city occupied by the Nazis and frequently bombed by the Allies where almost every street had fresh ruins, the sight of which brought misery to the grownups and joy to children and lost dogs looking for a place to hide. Strangely, even at the age of five I was not afraid of them like other people, but would approach them even when they appeared vicious and kept barking at me as if wanting to tear me apart. Since then I don't miss an opportunity to go over to a strange dog and introduce myself. By and large they tend to be lonely creatures and so am I. —*Charles Simic*

Dog on a Chain

So, that's how it's going to be,
A gray afternoon smelling of snow.
Step around the bare oak tree
And see how quickly you get
Yourself entangled for good?
Your bad luck was being friendly
With people who love their new couch
More than they love you.

Fred, you poor mutt, the night
Is falling. The children playing
Across the road were cold,
So they ran in. Watch the smoke
Swirl out of their chimney
In the windy sky as long as you're able.
Soon, no one will see you sitting there.
You'll have to bark even if
There's no moon, bark and growl
To keep yourself company.

Icarus's Dog

He let the whole world know
What he thought of his master's stunt.
People threw rocks at him,
But he went on barking.

A hot day's listlessness
Spread over the sea and the sky.
Not even a single gull
To commemorate the event.

Finally, he called it quits and went
To sniff around some bushes,
Vanishing for a moment,
Then reappearing somewhere else,

Wagging his tail happily as he went
Down the long, sandy beach,
Now and then stopping to pee
And take one more look at the sky.

LES MURRAY
(1938–2019)

Two Dogs

Enchantment creek underbank pollen, are the stiff scents he
    makes,
hot grass rolling and rabbit-dig but only saliva chickweed.
Road pizza clay bird, hers answer him, rot-spiced good. Blady
    grass,
she adds, ant log in hot sunshine. Snake two sunups back. Orifice?
Orifice, he wriggles. Night fox? Night fox, with left pad wound.
Cement bag, hints his shoulder. Catmeat, boasts his tail, twice
    enjoyed.
Folded sapless inside me, she clenches. He retracts initial blood.
Frosty darks coming, he nuzzles. High wind rock human-free
    howl,
her different law. Soon. Away, away, eucalypts speeding—
Bark! I water for it. Her eyes go binocular, as in pawed
hop frog snack play. Come ploughed, she jumps, ground. Bark
    tractor,
white bitterhead grub and pull scarecrow. Me! assents his urine.

The Fair Go

A ginger-biscuit kelpie dog,
young, abandoned off the highway
up a gravel road. Livestock
and rifle country, so the big
harp of ribs in its mouth
as its start in life is
butcher-cut. To prove innocence.

A Dog's Elegy

The civil white-pawed dog who'd strain
to make speech-like sounds to his humans
lies buried in the soil of a slope
that he'd tear down on his barking runs.

He hated thunder and gunshot
and would charge off to restrain them.
A city dog too alive for backyards,
we took him the pound's Green Dream

but now his human name melts off him;
he'll rise to chase fruit bats and bees;
the coral tree and the African tulip
will take him up, and the prickly tea trees.

Our longhaired cat who mistook him
for an Alsatian flew up there full tilt
and teetered in top twigs for eight days
as a cloud, distilling water with its pelt.

The cattle suspect the Dog lives
but three kangaroos stood in our pasture
this daybreak, for the first time in memory,
eared gazing wigwams of fur.

TOI DERRICOTTE
(b. 1941)

THIS POEM IS about Footsie, a beautiful and loving Norwegian
Elkhound who acted as something between a guiding angel and
a mother to me. She came into my life when my son was about
seven—to be discovered in a box under his bed for his Christmas
present—and stayed for almost fifteen years when she died. Once,
when she was a couple of years old, my son brought home a kit-
ten he had found on the railroad tracks. During the night I heard
strange sounds and, when I went to see, Footsie was nursing him.
In old age, when she was unable to walk up and down the stairs,
I carried her like a bride. I can hardly wait to hug her in heaven.
—*Toi Derricotte*

The Good Old Dog

I will lay down my silk robe
beside me near the old bed,
for the good old dog;
     she loves the feel
of it under her, and she will
push it and pull it, knead

and scrape until she has it right;
    then she'll drop down,
heavy, silver and black in the moonlight,
on it and a couple of pillows (not
bothering the cat who has taken over
    her real bed)

    and breathe out deeply.

Gorgeously fat,
her face
like the face of a seal.

HUGO WILLIAMS
(b. 1942)

DOGS ARE METAPHORS of course, like poems themselves,
woolly equations with humour. Sometimes I don't know which
side I'm on. Mine is not a great poem. Too abstract. No dogs to
be seen. Because no experience of dogs, only of writing about
them. Top-heavy equation but like my life in a way. I think I
just wanted to say "up on the downs" to remind me of my child-
hood and our dog called Slasher who preferred people to dogs.
—*Hugo Williams*

Memory Dogs

When I put on my coat they're all over me
to take them up on the downs
for games with sticks.
Their eyes follow me round the room.
When I reach for a book
they hang their heads in shame.

I took them to the outskirts of town
and opened the car door.

By the time I reached home
they were waiting on the doorstep for me.
Whatever made me think
I could live without them?

MICHAEL ONDAATJE
(b. 1943)

A Dog in Berkeley

Sitting in an empty house
with a dog from the Mexican Circus!
O Daisy, embrace is my only pleasure.
Holding and hugging my friends. Education.
A wave of eucalyptus. Warm granite.
These are the things I have in my heart.
Heart and skills, there's nothing else.

I usually don't like small dogs but you
like midwestern women take over the air.
You leap into the air and pivot
a diver going up! You are known
to open the fridge and eat when you wish
you can roll down car windows and step out
you know when to get off the elevator.

I always wanted to be a dog
but I hesitated
for I thought they lacked certain skills.
Now I want to be a dog.

CRAIG RAINE
(b. 1944)

As CHILDREN, WE put our first puppy down the bed and used it as a hot-water bottle.

Puppies: not long after a desolate, expensive, arranged coupling in a field outside Southampton, my son's Weimaraner bitch gave birth to eleven pups. The vet's prediction was two. They emerged at intervals like black puddings, tubes wrapped in cling film. The mother ate the Saran-wrap and the pups immediately acquired legs, ears, tails, movement and the temporary personality of Blind Pugh. They fed like the Eton Wall Game. She ate their poo. I was amazed by her instincts, her certainty.

And then their irresistible eyes appeared: "your yen two wol slee me soddenly; / I may the beautee of hem not sustene," as Chaucer puts it in his poem "Merciles Beaute."—*Craig Raine*

The Behaviour of Dogs
Their feet are four-leafed clovers
that leave a jigsaw in the dust.

They grin like Yale keys and tease
us with joke-shop Niagara tongues.

A whippet jack-knives across the grass
to where the afghan's palomino fringe

is part Opera House curtain, part
Wild Bill Hicock. Its head

precedes the rest, balanced like
a tray, aloft and the left.

The labrador cranks a village pump,
the boxer shimmies her rump,

docked to a door knocker, and
the Alsation rattles a sabre—

only the ones with crewcuts fight.
Sportif, they scratch their itches

like one-legged cyclists sprinting
for home, pee like hurdlers,

shit like weightlifters, and relax
by giving each other piggy backs . . .

Das Lied von der Erde

A hand of ginger, bulbous,
like the Willendorf Venus.

Exaggerated, accurate, gross.
Like these ugly, uncircumcised teats,

a Greek or Indian grocer's
unappetising, soiled carrots:

this bitch
with her ten hairy tits.

A litter of eleven strains
like the Eton Wall Game.

Brute tugs
at distended dugs.

(At full stretch, each one is
long as a monkey penis.)

Vaginal ooze,
vermilion glue,

elastic blood, brilliant,
thick as gloss paint.

Nothing lyric about birth
or after-birth.

Song of the earth.

Bitch

This Weimaraner in Spandex,
tight on the deep chest,
webbed at the tiny waist.

The drips and drabs of her dugs:
ten, a tapering wedge,
narrowed towards the back legs.

She gives me her paw,
a branch with buds, four
spare pads and claws.

Her tail's unstoppable verve
and swerve,
the long hard curve

of a skipping rope.
Metronomic, rapid,
slow, three-speed raps.
Each ear an evening dress
cut on the bias.
The golden eyes pious

(praying for food).
She poos
like a kangaroo.

Hunger: her muzzle's
cribbage board a drizzle
of glycerin spittle.

She sleeps as if
she were a penknife,
legs half-folded away. Twitched off.

And eats like a washing machine.
The lavish eight-inches-long
shoe-shop-shoehorn tongue.

CHRISTOPHER REID
(b. 1949)

I HAVE NEVER owned a dog, but I live in London where they are a vital part of the city's everyday carnival. Their earnestness, their ebullience, their commitment to the present moment, and their hunger for fun are just some of the qualities that enchant me. When I was commissioned to write *Old Toffer's Book of Consequential Dogs*, my canine response to Eliot's *Practical Cats*, it was not hard to find personalities to populate it with. My dogs came mobbing and nudging round me, demanding to be put into poems exactly as they might insist on being taken for walks.
—*Christopher Reid*

Dogs and Ghosts
for Molly Sackler

Over tea at the Algonquin,
  where, among the witty ghosts,
that of Thurber, who loved to draw dogs—
  themselves like the ghosts of dogs—
haunts the mid-afternoon shadows
  more livingly than most,

you asked me about my own
    dog-populated poems.
Why so many? I couldn't
    explain it then, but lately
bumping into a dog I know,
    who, to judge by her torpedo greeting,
seemed to know me too,
    I saw what might be a clue
in the oddity, the imbalance,
    the off-balance of our meeting.
With their intemperate dashes at the barrier
    that's fixed between the species,
their sharp offal-huff and slaver
    aimed towards our faces,
their paws scrabbling at our chests
    in high-minded yearning to be
of us, and not just with us,
    dogs now strike me
as champion four-legged metaphors
    for metaphors: their use,
in a certain kind of poem,
    to be true to a parallel destiny
at much the same distance as ghosts are,
    only yappy and footloose.

ANDREW MOTION
(b. 1952)

I WAS BROUGHT up in the countryside (East Anglia) and, although we never said as much, I think my parents, my brother and I all preferred animals to most people. Dogs especially, because they belonged to both the world outside us and to our own human world: they were in a sense strangers and therefore objects of interest, but also cosy and therefore our intimates. There was always a Labrador (my father's dog and meant to be tough, but always corrupted by our affection), and trotting alongside it "Mum's dog," which was never exactly a lap dog, but always ready to hop onto a lap if one was offered. From the age of 0 to 18, when I left home, both were my more or less constant holiday companions: spirit-raisers, sort-of confidantes, indispensable goofs.

These days it's cats I can't do without—their choosiness and their independence. Compared to these things, the optimism of dogs feels slightly depressing. Although I can still see that if it isn't stupid, there might be something heroic in dogs' ability to think the best of us. —*Andrew Motion*

The Dog of the Light Brigade

We have to remember when Raglan and others [1]
decided their moment for glory had come,
and ordered their mess-mates and countrymen –
yes, the noble six hundred, most of whom never

had even so much as imagined what shooting
and shelling were like away from the Shires,
much less endured it—when they had advanced them
up to the mouth of the innocent valley known later

thanks to the Laureate Alfred Lord Tennyson, [2]
thanks be to him, as the Valley of Death, the din
of their bugling and clanking, snorting and stamping,
stretched back to the stables a distance behind them,

and woke there the pampered fox terrier bitch
kept by the men as a mascot, who thinking that this
was the point of her madcap existence revealed at last,
sprang from her bed among tit-bits of horse-dung,

squeezed through a crack in the planks of a door,
then again through the wind-milling arms of a boy,

1. Motion refers to Field Marshal FitzRoy James Henry Somerset, 1st Baron Raglan, GCB, PC (1788–1855), commander of British troops in the Crimean War. He was responsible for the disastrous Charge of the Light Brigade on October 25, 1854, which he witnessed. 2. Poet Laureate Alfred, Lord Tennyson wrote "The Charge of the Light Brigade," published on December 9, 1854.

and sped off to join them. This was the creature
that nothing surprised in the barracks. Most nights,

indulged with a table-side seat in the mess, she gazed
on the rubicund faces of men whose acceptable practice
was drinking until one collapsed, whose whiskery mouths
repeated the same snorting farmyard of noises over and over,

viz: Frenchmen and Russians and women and Prussians
and Turks and women again, until they were cancelled
one by the other, or smudged in the baccy-smoke,
wine-fumes and high-collared heat of the moment,

but nothing, no nothing had ever prepared him
for this—for the firecracker racket that rattled
the air they rode into, the po-faced hilarious crash
of men who could empty an armful of bottles

straight off and not bat an eyelid, the antics
of horses in suddenly kneeling, or slithering
sideways, or stopping stock-still, which is why
she kept pace with them through to the cannon line,

bouncing the heathery turf and yapping her head off,
a black-and-white-blur at the corner of everyone's eye,
and then turning around when the rest of them also
turned round, and skittering back, bounding higher

this time to get clear of the men lying higgledy-
piggledy blocking her way, until losing patience,
and anyway puffed with the effort of running
(although the whole business had lasted fifteen or so

minutes at best), and then strutting off as though life
was the same, to the stables to sample a tit-bit of dung
she had saved, before a quick session of mousing,
and after that, falling asleep.

LAVINIA GREENLAW
(b. 1962)

OUR DOG WAS named after my great-grandfather, a Welsh chapel minister called Ebenezer Griffith-Jones. As a puppy he chewed on a small wooden dove of peace. He would bury bone-shaped dog-biscuits by placing them on the wooden floor and performing a gesture that connoted burial. We tried not to disturb them. When I felt unable to raise my head, he would lay his head beside mine. A sheepdog, he was compelled to herd buses along the village high street. Old and in pain, he slipped out and lay down in the road. His loyalty was so strong that his ghost persisted in turning up wherever you'd expect to find him. —*Lavinia Greenlaw*

For the First Dog in Space

You're being sent up in Sputnik 2,
a kind of octopus with rigor mortis.
Ground control have sworn allegiance
to gravity and the laws of motion;
they sleep without dreams,
safe in the knowledge
that a Russian mongrel bitch
can be blasted through the exosphere

at seven miles a second,
but can never stray far from home.
You will have no companion,
no buttons to press, just six days' air.
Laika, do not let yourself be fooled
by the absolute stillness
that comes only with not knowing
how fast you are going. As you fall
in orbit around the earth, remember
your language. Listen to star dust.
Trust your fear.

SIMON ARMITAGE
(b. 1963)

I'VE NEVER REALLY owned a dog (has anyone?). And on those
occasions when a dog has lived in the house it's never really been
mine. So my experience of dogs has been somewhat partial and
accidental, though I'm a dog fan, generally speaking, and believe
they usually appeal to the better parts of our nature. In observing
dogs I've always been more interested in their effect on their own-
ers than the animals themselves, not least the way dogs become
an externalised aspect of an owner's personality. The fact that this
relationship is played out without the use of language is especially
interesting to a poet. I've made lists of potential dog names with-
out really having any desire to acquire one, and my favourite so
far is Monday (a silver-grey rescue whippet, probably). —*Simon
Armitage*

Before you cut loose,
                          put dogs on the list
of difficult things to lose. Those dogs ditched
on the North York Moors or the Sussex Downs
or hurled like bags of sand from rented cars
have followed their noses to market towns

and bounced like balls into their owners' arms.
I heard one story of a dog that swam
to the English coast from the Isle of Man,
and a dog that carried eggs and bacon
and a morning paper from the village
surfaced umpteen leagues and two years later,
bacon eaten but the eggs unbroken,
newsprint dry as tinder, to the letter.
A dog might wander the width of the map
to bury its head in its owner's lap,
crawl the last mile to dab a bleeding paw
against its own front door. To die at home,
a dog might walk its four legs to the bone.
You can take off the tag and the collar
but a dog wears one coat and one colour.
A dog got rid of—that's a dog for life.
No dog howls like a dog kicked out at night.
Try looking a dog like that in the eye.

A. E. STALLINGS
(b. 1968)

An Ancient Dog Grave, Unearthed During Construction of the Athens Metro

It is not the curled-up bones, nor even the grave
That stops me, but the blue beads on the collar
(Whose leather has long gone the way of hides),
The ones to ward off evil. A careful master
Even now protects a favorite, just so.
But what evil could she suffer after death?
I picture the loyal companion, bereaved of her master,
Trotting the long, dark way that slopes to the river,
Nearly trampled by all the nations marching down,
One war after another, flood or famine,
Her paws sucked by the thick, caliginous mud,
Deep as her dewclaws, near the riverbank.
In the press for the ferry, who will lift her into the boat?
Will she cower under the pier and be forgotten,
Forever howling and whimpering, tail tucked under?
What stranger pays her passage? Perhaps she swims,

Dog-paddling the current of oblivion.
A shake as she scrambles ashore sets the beads jingling.
And then, that last, tense moment—touching noses
Once, twice, three times, with unleashed Cerberus.

ACKNOWLEDGMENTS

Dog-eared has many friends whom I wish to thank here: Gideon Nesbit from the University of Birmingham has shown generosity not only in approving of my rough and ready treatment of Martial but in bringing to my attention Crinagoras's "Dog Avoidance Tactics," and allowing me to use his rendering of it. Carolyne Larrington, Professor of Medieval European Literature at the University of Oxford, generously supplied me with her most up-to-date translation of the *Edda*, which appears in these pages. Tatiana Lebreton of the School of Oriental and African Studies (SOAS) in London was kind enough to respond to far too many questions about Victor Hugo's use of tone, as did my long-suffering Georgetown colleague Andrew Sobanet, Professor in the Department of French and Francophone Studies. Dr. Tom Walker, Ussher Assistant Professor in Irish Writing, Trinity College, Dublin, provided invaluable insider knowledge about Louis Macneice and his canine obsessions. Deirdre Le Faye alerted me to the existence of poems of which I was unaware. My Georgetown colleague John Hirsh reminded me of medieval hounds and lapdogs I would otherwise have overlooked; while friend and mentor Paul F. Betz lent me the manuscript of Byron's memorial to Boatswain.

Acknowledgments

I'm grateful to Shazia Amin for her meticulous and sympathetic copyediting, and to Connor Guy, my editor at Basic Books, for being an exemplary editor in every way. I'm grateful also to my agent Charlie Viney; Catherine Payling MBE; and Topsy the smooth fox terrier, a Texan with a zero-tolerance policy on squirrels. For frank exchanges on the authors and poems in this volume, I am grateful to Thomas Mann and his League of Extraordinary Gentlemen at the Cosmos Club in Washington, DC.

Fees or royalties received from sales of this book will be shared with the American Society for the Prevention of Cruelty to Animals (ASPCA) and the American Fox Terrier Rescue (AFTR).

Duncan Wu
Georgetown University
January 2020

PERMISSIONS

Grateful acknowledgment is made to the following authors, editors, heirs, publishers, and agents for their permissions to reprint poems in *Dog-eared*:

Fleur Adcock, "A Surprise in the Peninsula," from *Poems 1960–2000* by Fleur Adcock (Bloodaxe Books, 2000), Copyright © 2000 by Fleur Adcock.

Simon Armitage, "Before You Cut Loose," from *The Dead Sea Poems* by Simon Armitage (Faber and Faber, 1995), Copyright © 1995 by Simon Armitage. US: Reprinted with permission of David Godwin Associates; outside the US: Reprinted with permission of Faber and Faber.

Li Bai, "Visiting the Recluse on Mount Daitian and Not Finding Him In," translated by Stephen Owen, from *The Great Age of Chinese Poetry: The High Tang* by Stephen Owen, Copyright © 2013 by Stephen Owen and the Quirin Press, ISBN: 9781922169068 Paperback, Quirin Press 2013, p. 134.

Gwendolyn Brooks, "Vern," Copyright © 1957 by Gwendolyn Brooks. Reprinted with permission of Brooks Permissions.

Toi Derricotte, "The Good Old Dog," from *Captivity* by Toi Derricotte, Copyright © 1989. Reprinted with permission of the University of Pittsburgh Press.

T. S. Eliot, "Five Finger Exercises" no 2, and "Lines to a Yorkshire Terrier," from *Collected Poems 1909–1962* by T. S. Eliot, Copyright © 1963 by Faber and Faber.

Lawrence Ferlinghetti, "Dog," from *A Coney Island of the Mind* by Lawrence Ferlinghetti, Copyright ©1958 by Lawrence Ferlinghetti. Reprinted with permission of New Directions Publishing Corp.

Lavinia Greenlaw, "The First Dog in Outer Space," from *Night Photograph* by Lavinia Greenlaw (Faber and Faber, 1993), Copyright © 1993 by Lavinia Greenlaw. Reprinted with permission of Faber and Faber.

Permissions

Galway Kinnell, "Burning," from *Collected Poems of Galway Kinnell*, Copyright © 2017 by the Literary Estate of Galway Kinnell, LLC. Translated and reprinted with permission of Houghton Mifflin Harcourt Publishing Company. All rights reserved.

Louis Macneice, "Dogs in the Park," from *The Collected Poems of Louis Macneice*, Copyright © 1961 by the Estate of Louis Macneice. Reprinted with permission of David Higham.

Andrew Motion, "The Dog of the Light Brigade," from *Public Property* by Andrew Motion, Copyright © 2002. Reprinted with permission of Faber and Faber.

Les Murray, "Two Dogs," "The Fair Go," and "A Dog's Elegy" from *New Collected Poems* by Les Murray (Carcanet Press, 2003). Reprinted with permission of the Estate of Les Murray and Carcanet Press.

Howard Nemerov, "Walking the Dog," from *Sentences*, Copyright © 1980 by Howard Nemerov. Reprinted with permission of Alexander Nemerov and the Estate of Howard Nemerov.

Michael Ondaatje, "A Dog in Berkeley," previously entitled "A Dog in San Francisco" (changed by request of Mr. Ondaatje, who writes: "The owner of the dog complained she lives in Berkeley not San Francisco"), from *The Cinnamon Peeler: Selected Poems* by Michael Ondaatje, Copyright © 1997. Reprinted with permission of W. W. Norton and Trident Media Group.

Craig Raine, "The Behaviour of Dogs," "Das Lied von der Erde," and "Bitch," Copyright © 1978, 2019 by Craig Raine. Reprinted with permission of Craig Raine.

Christopher Reid, "Dogs and Ghosts," from *For and After* by Christopher Reid (Faber and Faber, 2003), Copyright © 2003 by Christopher Reid. Reprinted with permission of Faber and Faber.

Siegfried Sassoon, "Man and Dog," from *Collected Poems 1908–1956* (Faber and Faber, 1986), Copyright © 1986 by Siegfried Sassoon. Reprinted with permission of the Estate of George Sassoon.

Vernon Scannell, "Dead Dog," from *Collected Poems 1950–1993* (Robson Books, 1993), Copyright © 1993 by the Estate of Vernon Scannell. Reprinted with permission of the Estate of the late Vernon Scannell.

Frederick Seidel, "The Little White Dog," from *Poems 1959–2009* by Frederick Seidel, Copyright © 2009 by Frederick Seidel. Reprinted with permission of the Wylie Agency LLC.

Charles Simic, "Dog on a Chain" and "Icarus's Dog," from *Night Picnic: Poems by Charles Simic*, Copyright © 2001 by Charles Simic. Reprinted with permission of Houghton Mifflin Harcourt Publishing Company. All rights reserved.

AUTHOR'S NOTE

I thank the people who helped me as I gathered permissions to reprint: Frederick T. Courtright, President, The Permissions Company, LLC; Catherine Green, Trident Media Group; Suzanne Fairless-Aitken, Bloodaxe Books; Adrienne Gwozdecky, The Wylie Agency; Alicia M. Dercole, Senior Associate, Permissions, Penguin Random House; Courtney Smotherman, Assistant to the Director, Northwestern University Press; Ron Hussey, Director of Permissions, HMH Books & Media; Christopher Wait, Permissions Editor, New Directions Publishing; Pamela Williams, Client Services Manager, Brooks Permissions; Vicki Salter, Barbara Levy Literary Agency; Johanna Clarke, David Higham Associates; Michael Schmidt OBE FRSL, Carcanet Press Ltd.; Alexander Nemerov, Carl and Marilynn Thoma Provostial Professor in the Arts and Humanities, Stanford University; Martin Reed on behalf of the Estate of Vernon Scannell; Eileen L. O'Malley, Operations Administrator, University of Pittsburgh Press; William Siskin, Quirin Press; and Hattie Cooke at Faber and Faber; as well as the following authors: Christopher Reid, Michael Ondaatje, Craig Raine, Hugo Williams, Lavinia Greenlaw, Simon Armitage, Toi Derricotte, Charles Simic, and Andrew

Motion. I am greatly indebted to Alex Colston of Basic Books and Keenan Clark of Georgetown University for assistance in tracing copyright holders, and to Karen Lautman, senior administrator in my department at Georgetown, for being so efficient in her handling of permissions.

Charlie Glover

Duncan Wu is Raymond A. Wagner professor of literary studies at Georgetown University, a former fellow of St. Catherine's College, Oxford, and a former professor of English Literature at the University of Glasgow. He has written on Romantic writers from William Wordsworth to William Hazlitt, as well as on contemporary British theater and the American Beat Generation. He became an American citizen in 2013 and lives with his wife, Catherine Payling, MBE, and Topsy the Dog in McLean, Virginia. Topsy is a smooth fox terrier rescued by the Fox Terrier Network of North America—which, with the ASPCA, will benefit from sales of this book.